Invisible Driving

Alistair McHarg

ISBN : 1-4196-5447-0

To order additional copies, please contact us.
BookSurge, LLC
www.booksurge.com
1-866-308-6235
orders@booksurge.com

Invisible Driving

Acknowledgements

My brother Malcolm, who, like the rest of us, didn't expect the Spanish Inquisition. Alex Stiber, progenitor, connoisseur, fellow Eulipian. Steven Samuel, Ph.D., sage counsel through the labyrinth of recovery. Dan Endicott, artiste extraordinaire. Nancy Biddle, graphics diva. Anne Kaier, poet, advocate, impresaria. Haldy Gifford, poultry portraitist, marketing guru, comrade. John Schuster, Jennifer Ballard, and the entire BookSurge team. Most important, the lovely and talented Lisa Dee, my right arm in all endeavors.

"Perhaps everything that is terrible is in its deepest being something helpless that wants help from us."

Rainer Maria Rilke
Letters To A Young Poet

This book is dedicated to my daughter Paula.

Chapter 1

The Empty Car

These are glory days for Invisible Driving. I've discovered the core position, The Empty Car. While performing The Empty Car I'm in the driver's seat with feet on pedals in the normal arrangement but all of me above waist level is bent over, resting on the passenger's seat. I have the mirrors set so that I can still see perfectly well but to all observers the car is unoccupied. It's incredibly funny. We're talking radnopolis funny. Impossible for me to pull this maneuver without cracking up into a squizzling, snerchified hysterical laughter. I laugh with a nervous, giddy delight at the sheer absurdity of it. I laugh with a childish delight at the outrageousness of it. I laugh with an anxious excitement, agitated by the risk. But I laugh most uncontrollably as I imagine the reactions of the passengers in the cars who see this apparition. The ghost car. This is my only regret, that I never get to hear the comments of the people who have this performance foist, and the foist shall be last and the last shall be foist, upon them. How does one react when one confronts the thing which cannot be? Eh? See? If, as a teenager, you ever mooned a busload of senior citizens, that is, exposed your naked behind to them from a moving automobile, you have an idea of some of the facial expressions I encounter when I reemerge from my crouch. Contempt. Shock. Surprise. Extippitox squatchifromp. Amazement. Naturally it's the kids who enjoy it most. Unlike so many of the adults who try to ignore this inexplicable phenomenon, the kids point, laugh, jump up and down, and stare. Once, I slowed down at a stoplight after a particularly long stretch of invisibility to find myself, which was an enormous relief because I'd been looking for myself everywhere, being applauded by a carload of black youths. It's not unusual for cars to follow me for miles as though their drivers are trying to reconfirm that they are indeed seeing what they think they're seeing. An empty car driving down the road, obeying speed limits and other traffic regulations. I've started to see some of the same cars with a certain regularity. They follow me, forming a kind of train. Talk about building a following, talk about squazmogrified pontippelation. Taking my show on the road. This invention will certainly cinch my claim to fame, and the fortune that comes along with it. If it's ever been done before I'm certainly unaware of it. Surely such a unique, delightful, original gift to society deserves compensation.

Downtown Invisible Driving is the most difficult but provides the biggest rewards. Though my hyper-awareness, my sensitivity to everything going on around me, makes it easier it's still a risky occupation but isn't greatness always risky, it's only mediocrity that offers no challenge. I don't want to ruin the fun by getting into an accident, or worse, being stopped by a policeman. So the stretches of Invisible Driving are short, short, but effective. A quick swoop down Chestnut Street during lunch hour is always successful. Lots of pedestrians. One notices, stops in his or her tracks, and sets off a whole wave of wonder. If George Bush was prancing down the street naked I can't imagine there would be more dropped jaws. I'm also fond of driving up to my favorite spots at night, the hotels where there are always doormen and people coming in and out. I pull up very slowly, the black Volvo sedan, clean, conservative, quiet, purring up to the door, stealthy, driverless. I let the patrons get a good look and then cruise on. It's wonderful, so goddamn funny I can't believe it. A legend is being born. A modern day equivalent of the headless horseman of Sleepy Hollow.

As the last days of January evaporate like snow from a sidewalk I hone and refine my repertoire. I told Claire about my discovery. She found it inspired, thinking of it in terms of performance art. With her permission, I rummaged through her workroom for props. Jackpot. Claire, who loves odd things and never throws anything away, has some bizarre artifacts, among them, a pair of Mickey Mouse hands. Rather, huge, white, plastic gloves. I use these, and one of her mannequins, in Invisible Driving stunts. The Mickey Mouse gloves serve in the Invisible Driving position I call, Look Ma, No Hands. I drive the car by steering with my knees and slip on the plastic hands. Then I hold up the enormous white gloves so that everyone can see that I'm driving without using my hands. There are many ways to drive a car and some of them are legal. I make elaborate use of them for hand signals, indicating a right turn by sticking my right arm out of the passenger's window. Or, I hold them both up, palms forward, and rock them back and forth in tandem like twin pendulums on a demented cuckoo clock. If I'm not satisfied that I'm generating enough interest I stick them both out the window, left hand out of left window and right hand out of right window, and grip the roof as though if I let it go it will come flying off. This makes it clear to even the least astute observer that I'm driving without the use of my hands.

The mannequin makes it possible to perform, The Invisible Chauffeur. I set Claire's mannequin up in the back seat, always careful to strap her in with the three-point seat belt. Safety first. Unfortunately Claire didn't have a wig for her. Small surprise there, what Claire spends on cosmetics in a year wouldn't pay my bar tab at the Four Seasons for a week. However I do have a sweater, scarf, and coat for her, and a hat. From a distance she's convincing enough. And that's what it's all about. Illusion. Combine The Empty Car with a mannequin in the back seat and I have, The Invisible Chauffeur. This goes over particularly well at The Four Seasons, The Bellevue, and The Rittenhouse, all of which have highly visible approaches to their front doors. A woman sitting in the back seat of a conservative car, being driven to the door of a luxury hotel, is a commonplace sight.

But on closer examination, the car has no driver. Why does the woman seem so composed, given these circumstances?

After a while the doormen at these places got the idea and they get quite a kick out of it. If there are patrons around they act appropriately disinterested but if it's just them they laugh, drag their coworkers out of the hotel to catch a look, holler at me to come in, generally sign on. They get it. They're on the bus. They're street level, real people. I feel a kinship with them, we're all in this together. They know I'm doing publicly what they do privately, mock the world they have to take seriously, the world of chauffeurs, the world of show furs, opulence, leisure. I'm becoming an underground celebrity which must explain why I'm coffin. McHarg, the only man to become famous by becoming invisible. But it's not my aim to become famous, this is just something to amuse myself, and others, until stardom shows up at my door, relieved to have found me at last. I have an enormous appetite for entertainment, and a very short attention span.

Perhaps the most obscure of all the Invisible Driving positions is, A Day In The Life Of Isadora Duncan. This one is for double bonus points. I'm always wearing scarves, a stylish fashion accessory which I employ, though unemployed myself I am an employer, to maximum effect. I take the longest one, a wool number with a bright, predominately red Tartan, and gradually feed it out the window when another car is next to me. As it begins to whip in the wind I feed it out more until at last it stretches practically to the back of the car. By then, of course, I have the attention of the people in the car next to me. When I'm certain I have their full notice, and not just their thirty-day notice, I clutch my throat as though the scarf is choking me, pulling me out of the car. I panic, bug-eyed, making quite a production of it. At last I lay my head out of the window, tongue drooping ominously, like a dead deer. Are there any liberal arts majors out there who get this one? I don't know. If there are, I hope they'll save the last dance for me.

It's For You is an Invisible Driving position in response to the popularity of car phones. Car phones are starting to become commonplace and I marvel at the self-important way that people use them, making sure to let everyone see that they have one. What could be so important that it can't wait until they get home, or back to the office? It makes them feel important, and above all, productive in an upwardly mobile sort of way, to use a car phone. I took one of the phones from my house, since the service has been shut off there isn't much else to do with them, and put it in my car. I spot some hot shot jabbering away on his car phone and I start jabbering away too, pretending to be talking to somebody. I shadow the car, staying right next to him in the adjoining lane so that we both stop at a traffic light at the same time. Then I honk my horn to get his attention and when I do, motion for him to roll down his window. This invariably provokes irritation and confusion. What fun. What squatch. What kind of fool am I, that likes to mess with heads? Mixing it up with the reptiles. Running circles round the squares. In most cases the person, nearly always a man, relents and rolls down the passenger's side window. When he does I offer my phone to him and say with a totally deadpan expression, "It's for you." Anger, scowls, eyes rolling upwards towards heaven, unless of course heaven is not above in which case they're merely rolling upwards towards the air pollution, the reactions are predictable. One guy did laugh. Another guy earned himself a permanent place in my personal pantheon by looking at me and cool as an assassin saying, "Just take a message and have him call me back." That one cracked me up and God knows that doesn't happen often enough. Bless the ones who get the joke and bless the ones who get on the bus.

As I drive invisibly I do a play-by-play monologue, as though I'm describing a ball game. "Now it's an empty car. Now it's a car with a person in the front passenger seat but no driver. I can't believe I'm doing this with no hands. Now it's a car being driven by a very, very, very short man. Now it's a car being driven by a man with Mickey Mouse hands, and they're not on the wheel." The more I talk about it, the more rapanoochie it becomes. Of course, whenever I see a cop, I snap back into regulation status. "Now it's a car being operated normally."

One of the most challenging of the positions is, Nail It. Claire has taken to painting my toenails for some reason. God knows how long she's had the nail polish. Say God, how long has she had the nail polish? No answer. I rest my case. I don't think she has a message in it, rather, she just finds it a pleasant, hedonistic activity. A means of pampering that most neglected, hard working appendage, the foot. And, a splendid way to cap off an afternoon of toe sucking. So, in addition to a host of other quirks, including Rahsaan Roland Quirk, that one is for double bonus points, I'm now traipsing around town with bright purple toenails. When inclined, and even on level stretches of road, but folks, I remove my shoe and sock from my left foot and stick my left leg out the driver's window and into the bitter, winter air. It's difficult. The leg has to stretch quite a bit to do it. And in a car with a clutch, I always have to be ready to get the leg back inside at a moment's notice in case I need to change gears. Awareness is key, but for the effect to work, I have to appear relaxed. Not an easy stunt and worthy of my growing acumen which I'd planted in the back yard and watered regularly. When I perform this one I'm careful to point out to the usually appalled spectators that my toenails are painted. I need them to know that I go the extra distance for them. After all, it's details like these that separate the near great from the masters.

My intent is merely to delight. I discovered Invisible Driving one day and having discovered it I revel in it. I'm the soul of generosity, giving the world a unique gift. I'm certain that many of the drivers and pedestrians who witness these bizarre stunts are angered by my recklessness but there are others who understand. There's no harm intended, least of all to others. This is humor. Not ethnic slur humor, not toilet humor. Concept humor. A sliver of divine absurdity slipped into an otherwise average day. Something to make you laugh, so we can both laugh.

Invisible Driving does have a dark side too, but this is not for public consumption. The dark side slithers out of the swamp in the middle of the night, on abandoned roads, when there are no people around to entertain. There are Invisible Driving positions that have an audience of one, just me. Positions like Stealth Bomber, where my car is guided by moonlight only, all lights having been switched off. Positions like Ray Charles, where navigation is by sound alone. And the ultimate in Invisible Driving, Ray Charles—Stealth Bomber Pilot. If my heart is beating, I must still be alive.

Chapter 2

It's Just Got To Be That Way

Manic Depression almost destroyed me. It might still. There's no cure.

I live every single day of my life with the fear of becoming that man again. The man behind the wheel.

I'm never totally safe. I can't ever completely relax. I can't take my sanity for granted the way other people do.

I've gotten the upper hand. I had to, to survive. I've got a shrink. I take my Lithium. Every morning. Every evening. I've put together a support network of friends and family. The people I love can tell in a shot if I'm about to go off. They jump into action.

I'm trying not to be bitter. The ounce of prevention makes my life livable, but it doesn't cure anything. A couple of false steps and I'm back on shaky ground.

I hate this disease. I hate it. I hate it. I hate it. I hate it. I think about it every day, whether I want to or not. I couldn't add up what it's cost me. I couldn't measure how it's hurt me. It's stolen any chance I had for a normal life. My revenge is in hurting it back. I want to put a whoopin' on it, I want to kick its butt into the middle of next week.

I thought I was a real clever guy. I thought that by writing a book about Manic Depression I could loosen its grip on me once and for all. Look it in the eye like a man and stare it down. I thought that Manic Depression was an alligator and I was going to kill it and slice it up for shoes. For a while it did work out that way. I began to relax. Got a little cocky. I dozed off.

Then some stress at home and BAM, minor episodes began breaking out like a rash. They're easy to treat, but that doesn't make them fun.

When I build up a little confidence, the illness cuts me off at the knees. When I'm glad, it returns with a reason to be sad and scared. It seems like I'm always starting from scratch. Again. Again. Again.

This is the story of one of my three major Manic episodes. In many ways it was the worst one. I wrote it from the inside out because I wanted to blow the whistle on this pox. I wanted to give my readers an advantage my friends and family never had. Knowledge. It goes inside the Manic mind, inside the cracked logic. It reverberates with the sound of Manic speech. It sees the behavior through the eyes of the afflicted.

I've suffered because of this illness, really suffered. My friends, my family, they've suffered too. I want to redeem that suffering and make it worth something.

The telling takes you through the whole trip, with your tirelessly chatty narrator guiding the way. Beware of him. He's as far from me as Mars is from Mercury. I can't say I like him, but I do look on him with awe. Wonder. Even now, many years later, I can hardly believe it was me. But it was. I'm not proud of it. I'd pay the devil to be able to take it all back. But that luxury isn't an option. What remains is telling the truth of it.

When I was "high," Manic high, one of the dangerous things about me was that I believed my own twaddle. That gave me a power over people. My energy, creativity, and complete self-confidence were seductive. I was a tidal wave, pulling people into my delusions.

The episode was kick-started when my department at Honeywell was killed. Restructuring, downsizing, rightsizing, whatever you call it, it was corporate political gangland-style execution to me. A really wonderful department, full of great people. That was the best job I ever had, and I've had plenty. It had taken me a lot of sweat to get it, a lot of sweat, and a lot of heart.

I'd had to battle back from my first true Manic episode, that one was touched off by a really horrible divorce. Divorce *and* finding out that I was Manic Depressive, either one would have been enough by itself. That was a season in Hell. I was fired from jobs, found new ones, got fired from them too, all thanks to the illness.

At last I managed to pick myself up off the canvas and stop the stars from circling my head. I'd fought like hell to get a good custody agreement. I had a great relationship with my daughter Paula, she got every drop of love I had. I didn't have a girlfriend in those days so it was just me and the P, we were like a couple of buddies. I was devoted to her, I cared passionately about being a good father. My life was coming together, I was feeling security for the first time in my post-divorce life. I was pretty happy, even content. I felt that I'd become a man at last, independent and competent. Losing the job put an end to that.

A Manic episode can elevate instantly. One night I was washing the china, the next night I *was* China. For months after I was desperately racing. Going nowhere. Going off.

My mind glowed like a rocket, wildly churning out ideas. The ideas were totally unconnected, or, at best, hinged on a sliver of wordplay. At first this made me feel powerful, it's unbelievably entertaining. After a while, it was like having a demented television set in my brain that I couldn't turn off.

Chapter 3

Everything Is

Everything is the way it is for a reason. Or it isn't. Or both. Or neither. It's so hard to tell. It's so hard to tell you. But I can tell you. I can tell you a mile away. I can tell you're a mile away by the Luke in your eyes. I can tell you're a mile away by the Luke of the Irish. Irished everything for you, and this is the thanks I get? Thanks Igette, and thanks Igor, for a monstrous time. A monstrous hat was timed by all. All's well that's oiled well. Well oil right. Yes, oil right you when I get work. The abbey of Get Sesame. Get Seth and me. They're gonna come for me. They're gonna comfort me. They're gonna come fit me. Here cummerbund, marching down her street, stamp in defeat. Detail. The lust shall be first. Lust in space. The vet space the dogs because he has to, and he has three cats. Three cats, know weighting. The ting about that bell is the sound. The whole ting. Speaking of the Grand Canyon as a whole. He's holed up in the square. They squared off in the best circles. If you think the party is dull, circulate, if you think it's fun, circle seven. I've never seen you be four, I've seen you be three, but never be four. Nein! Ate. Severance. Sex. Thighs. Fore. Free. Toute. Won. Glasnost. Gezundheit! Ten Q. You're will's come. Where there's a will there's relatives. Come hear. Come overhear. He was overherd to say, "The cattle drink the milk." You herd me, ow. The cat had whiskers under his knows, he was pusstachioed. Whisker offer feet. Offer hand, knocker socks off. I'll besieging you, in old, familiar places. Place his everyone. Every won played Counts. Except those who played Contessas. The Count's divorce was uncontessad. That's wad he said. She bitter, man. At the auction she was chomping at the bid. Bitter farewell. Bidder farewell. Fair thee well, my own true's darning, four eyes am bound, and gagged, for old Virginny, Ginny, Ginny, Ginny, won't you take a rite with me, you've got the write stuff, bay B, you're the reason why I swing this scone, butter jam, jammer but, Chuck a Kong, Chuck a Kong, I've veal for you, I think olive you, I think all of you, fillings, nothing more than fillings, filling her up, feeling her down, she's a duck, DUCK! Imagine if your brrrr rain was bubbling like this constantly, do you think it might drive you bozznit after a while away the ours, what's Uri's is Uri's and what's Mayan is Mayan, Abyssinia, Sarong. "What sarong, is she wearing?" asked the seamstress. Clean up your asp. "How ya dune, Sandy?" "Not too Baghdad." The subway in London is the fellow peon tube. Tube B or not Tube B? I once met a Jewish gangster who was living in exile in the islands, his name was Bermuda Schwartz. Help! How do you turn this thing off? It's your turnip bat, Europe. European? No, it's just ice in my pocket. Pa kit, Ma kit, and locket. Let's go to Ma kit. The whole kitten kapoodle. Don't step in the poodles. She was only a stableman's daughter, but all the horsemen knew her. Then there was the performance artist who said, "I don't know much about art, but I know what I'm like." Power corrupts, absolute power corrupts Albert Finney. Remember that bastard Lester Maddox? He was a racist, and a brutal hatemonger. He was the Lester of two evils. And how about those Arab women, pretty in tents. When Arabs give gifts, do they do it in the present tents? Did you hear about the self-help book for architects, I.M. Pei, U.M. Pei? Help! Being in jail's not that bad, at least you don't have to agonize over vacation plans. Ahhh. Why do WASPs go to the hospital? For the food. Uhhh. If Sally Wong and Charlie Wong had a child, why wouldn't it be a Caucasian? Because two Wongs don't make a white. Stop, I'm killing me. Liquor, I hardly know her. How do you turn this thing off? Want a drink? No thanks, I'm not drinking any more.

Of course, I'm not drinking any less either. Chez When. Chez What? Ceasar. Ceasar what? Ceasar Chavez. Where is it? The streetcars are broken, there's sick transit on this glorious Monday. Ghengis Khan but Emmanual Kant. If I had it to do all over again, I'd do it all over you. My wife, give her an inch and she thinks she's a ruler. A hard man is good to find. I never metaphor I didn't like. You can lead a horticulture but you can't make her think. It's a boar ring case. Everybody has to believe something, I believe I'll have another drink. No matter where you go, there you are. The place is getting so popular, nobody goes there anymore. I can't go without Bea. I can't believe her behind. If you laid all the Freshmen girls at Bryn Mawr College end to end it wouldn't surprise me at all. Parker, I hardly know her. Yiiikes. There's no end insight. There's no big inning in sight either in this whole knew ballgame. The mice were so poor they could barely Eeeek out a living. Some of the snakes in India are so poor they don't have a pot to hiss in. Mints words, what the gay waiter spoke when dinner was over, done. When asked what was good on the menu the sarcastic waiter replied, "What's fair is fowl." "Through which canal passes the most food, Holmes?" "Alimentary my dear Watson." Give that lady barber more money, razor salary. Celery stalks at midnight. Noses run in my family. Days of whine and neuroses. I'm filing my nails under N. Under the broadwalk, down by the sea, at a banquet on my bay, Bea, that's where I'll be. The mentally ill comedian went sailing and was funny in the head. Stop. Where are the brakes? I could've become a race car driver but I never got the breaks I needed. And now the weather, fair today, unfair tomorrow. 101 Crustaceans. Lady and the Pimp. Snow White and The Trouble With Noses. Dumbro. Herbie The Love Slug. Bambi Does Bayonne. The Nutty Anesthesiologist. Disney or didn't he? Or, we could Duke it out, Take The Atrium. Louis Armstrong and Elephant Gerald. The prostitutes and the other convicts were having their annual checkup, the prison doctor was weighing the pros and the cons. There's no one else here, it's justice dear. How about the new alternative to those expensive scents in the stores, Eureka Cheap Perfume. Tequila Mockingbird. I'll see you insane Luis. Miss Anne Thrope was a guitarist, she used a misanthropic. My brain's throwing up, some pretty weird stuff, some old, some new, some borrowed, some blew right through the roof, I'm too chicken to get a cap on it. If I was the fatman of the opera I could put a capon it. When it's foggy by the shore it's bellwether for all sheeps at sea. There's a lot more in storm for ewe. When French people visit big Ben it's a froggy day in London town. Dracula was kicked out of college for having a bat attitude. A farmer in Idaho grew phallic shaped spuds and is marketing them as dictators. She used to work at the supermarket, she's an exchequer. Really, you can bank on it. If you've gotta run, you need new stockings. Jewish people who observe rituals even though it pains them to do it are Seder-masochists. If there's one thing I can't stand it's sitting. Poverty, the only thing money can't buy. Drunk tanks for the memories. I'm cold, so brrr. When the two writers argued at the Frick you could almost feel the fiction. Slowly the mortician turned the coroner. Although I put my foot in my mouth, I impediment what I said. I'm falling, leaf me in peace! I'm caught in the brain without an umbrella! He doesn't have enough sense to come in out of the brain. The mean Marine was rotten to the corps. On the Main Line, outside Philadelphia, when the evening sun is just right, you can see the amber graves of Wayne. My mind has a mind of its own and yes I do mind very much. But I don't mind the store. I'm not saying I like it, mind you. Mind you don't forget. My own thoughts are like a mind battlefield. Drinking volatility. Drug my own grave situation. I'm living in a house designed by Frank Lloyd Wrong. Give my complaints to the chef. Sing! I cant. Act! I get stuck in the wrong line. You recite for sore eyes. The wreck of the Titanic is hull king. It's not oeuvre 'till the fat lady sinks. A mind is a terrible thing to baste. I'll go to sea for myself. I'm sin King. They all laughed when I sat down to play the potato. Thank God, it's drawing to a clothes closet. I couldn't bare it, much languor. I've got a head full of ideas that are driving me, I'll delineate, driving me, driving me, driving me. There must be some kind of way out of here, bobbing along. Lead us not into Penn Station but deliver us from eagles. I can't turn this thing off. Chaka Khan. Out the door he goes. Slam goes the screen. Rabazibby.

Chapter 4

Killing Time Is Killing Me

My life today is pretty conventional. Together with my gorgeous girlfriend I own a small home in a sleepy suburb of Philadelphia. We've formed a blended family, her two kids and my one. A second chance for us all, refugees of divorce that we are. It's a worthy struggle. It has the messiness of real living, real passion.

Five days a week I drag myself to a job I hate. It's killing me an inch at a time. I'm a writer in a really pitiful Marketing Communications department. At other companies I've worked with people who were truly excellent. The best. I've been blessed with good teachers and I know my craft. I could do better. I should do better. I'm wasting my precious time there.

The worst of it is, I've been at it for almost five years. I stay because it's a steady paycheck. I've learned the hard way what that means. It means food. It means shelter. It means you get to live. I'm not a kid anymore, I can't afford to play games.

On the other hand, I'm proud that I've managed to hang on to one job for so long. Considering I'm Manic Depressive, that's more than a small accomplishment.

I'm the eldest of two sons. Like a lot of sons, I loved my mom with a love that was almost worship. And she really loved me. From her I learned what love is, how it's done, what it feels like. I was just twenty-four when she died. She lost a battle with leukemia that began when I was still in high school.

Losing her cut my legs out from under me. I drifted into a cold fog of depression that hung like a black shroud. I was so struck down and shaken that plenty of times I went to sleep in my clothes and wore them all the way through the next day. I just didn't give a shit about anything. It felt like the end, it felt like the joy had been sucked out of life itself.

A lot of time groaned by before I finally got the picture, before I finally understood how badly I'd been crippled by her cruel, cruel battle with cancer. I'd watched her eaten away, her own blood transformed into a demented river of agonized, toxic sleep. Eternal sleep. Racing madly to the ICU. Always needles, (she hated needles). Her brave smile. Experimental treatments. The loss of independence. The loss of dignity. Those damn hospital gowns. The laugh that all her friends knew her by, that signature, robust laugh, heard less and less. The way the nurses admired and loved her because she was so charming, so easy, no matter how bad the pain got.

God damn this fucking bitch of a world. That's how I felt. Samuel Beckett was right, everything adds up to nothing. The light glimmers for an instant, then it's gone, sucked into the cold vortex of black space. I hate everything. That's how I felt. I wanted to burn every tree, I wanted to black out the sun and make the whole world as cold as I felt. The planet was crawling with human refuse, people who were truly evil, why did God have to take her? And why in His so-called infinite wisdom did he have to torture her first?

When she was very ill I told her, "If I ever have a daughter, I'm going to name her after you." I felt so powerless in the face of her suffering, I wanted to do something that would make her happy, if only for a moment.

Years later, on the most joyful day of my life, my extraordinary daughter was born and I fulfilled that promise. More than anything else, that act, and the love and dedication which grew from it, reintroduced hope and happiness into my heart. It reconnected me to humanity. The love I have for my daughter is the best thing about me. The love I have for my daughter is my favorite thing about myself.

Lately she's taken to saying that she has my mother's spirit. If she's right, she's lucky, because she's got the noblest spirit I've ever known.

Like a lot of sons, I had a father who worked like a demon and wasn't at home much. He was very successful in his field. In my young eyes he was larger than life. He was Manic Depressive, with an unusual twist, he was Manic all the time. He had the poisonous heirloom, passed down to me like a witch's curse. Pray God, not to my daughter. The genes, the bent genes that flow through generations, spreading misery wherever they surface. I was scared of him. He was so big, so intense, so competent. Always competitive, with a fierce rage and a short temper.

He was a genius. Creative, original, spellbinding. He cast a giant shadow. I had to grow up in it. Escaping that shadow and getting into the light took a lot of damn walking. Friends have told me it's a miracle I survived growing up in his shadow at all.

I was raised in a sedate Philadelphia neighborhood called Chestnut Hill. My parents weren't rich, just comfortable. I went straight through school without any major problems, I made good grades, I was popular. I grew tall and strong. A gentle giant with a craggy face that seemed to be brooding. Summers in Ontario spent camping and canoeing kept me in good shape. My looks were good enough. A casual observer wouldn't have guessed that I was short on self-esteem.

My parents gave me a first-rate education. I owe them big time for that, I reap the rewards of that incredible gift every day. The love of culture, thought, imagination, has nourished me ever since. It's sustained me when my stuff got raggedy. I ran with a pack of guys who liked to think they were bad. In fact, we were about as bad as buttermilk cake. We devoted most of our energy to cars, cigarettes, alcohol, music, parties, and trying to get girls to notice us.

My parents came over after the war to go to school. They met in Cambridge, at a dance for foreign students. My mom was attending Radcliffe, my dad was at Harvard. He was originally from Clydebank, a working class community outside

Glasgow. My mom was from Amsterdam. She grew up in a very elite family environment, lots of servants, the whole thing. Her father helped found the World Bank. He was the Treasurer for years. But even though my mother's family was patrician, they were deep, ethical people.

Growing up in Amsterdam when it was occupied by the Nazis, watching friends taken away to be executed, my mom chose to join the Resistance. Together with her family, she hid Jews and Allied soldiers in her posh home for the entire duration of the war. The penalty for this was instant death, everyone knew it.

That idealism takes my breath away. The morality and courage of that brave, young woman makes me so proud of her I could cry. It's a beacon to me, it reminds me how people behave when they're at their very best.

Even though they were both young, my parents already had some horrifying history behind them when they moved to America for keeps in 1956. My mother's war experiences, my father's six years in the British Army. Like that whole wave of immigrants, they came determined to find their dream of a new, better life. Part of that dream involved giving their firstborn, their son, an idyllic, bourgeois, All-American childhood.

But even with all that going for me, I was a reserved young fellow. At times, a victim of depression. unaggressive, not competitive. The fear of my father became a fear of any authority. I liked the mental challenges of school but wasn't comfortable with personal challenges. I didn't have the appetite for blood sport. If I won, I felt like the other person wouldn't like me anymore. If I lost, I was stuck with the shame of defeat. And that was out because for some reason I'd gotten the idea that my parents, especially my dad, expected me to be perfect all the time.

I never had the gumption to grab life by the tie and demand what I wanted. To work harder. To want it more. Push past other people and just plain win. My moxie deficiency made me a, "Yes, honey," kind of husband. After my divorce I went to singles bars and struggled to cough up the courage I needed. Fear of rejection. Fear of happiness.

This unpalatable confession helps chart the vast ocean which separates my Manic persona from my day-to-day self. It's a strong testament to the power of the sickness. I've been too scared to dream. The Manic me just grabs. I've got genuine admiration and respect for women. My Manic self treats them like human toys. I dread attention, he demands it.

It was hideous to discover what I was capable of doing. Almost as if, when I was ill, I became all the things I feared and hated most.

Chapter 5

Let's Get Busy

Okay. Ready? Good. Let's get to it. Time to drop the needle in the tracks and separate the soul from the wax. Decided on a trip to D.C. do you see? Hang around with friends, formulate a plan, check in with two kittens I was grooming. Made calls, set dates, packed my papers up, blueprints for the life I was designing, rocket Metroliner down the northeast corridor to the bacon of industrial democracy.

Straight to the tail of the train for a joint, watched the rails whip away, like a pair of shiny serpents parallel. Over, I thought, it was over, and overrated by me, the life I wasn't living was over, glossy Metroliner, limos would be next. Everything awaited my arrival.

Sat alone, train mostly empty, or partly full, depending on perspective, as is the case with everything, gazed through glass at the green scenic smear, felt the electricity percolate my blood, girl came by, said it was her seat, said she'd only gone to get a soda. Automatic gentleman apologies. Second thoughts, minute thoughts, of hours spent together in secluded, romantic b and b's. Kiss, don't telephone, don't television. Asked her could I stay and she said, wood eye? Struck dumb stunned and amazed. Beauty so exquisite that it pained me, looks that were the fortune of a noble family, inherited like chairs by Duncan Phyfe. Blonde hair, blue eyes, strong cheekbones, thin nose, pouty lips, something almost tough in her persona. The body couldn't ever be as perfect as her face, but it was, especially the legs. Probably in her thirties, but dressed for an exclusive boarding school, crisp white blouse, suspenders, culottes, black watch plaid. Central casting fantasy, magic realized. How could I survive a life where dreaming made it so? The mettle I was made of was tested by her legs, I couldn't keep my eyes off of them.

Had a man-to-man conversation with myself, which left me with a few men to spare. You want to hit on her, that's apparent, but you're on your way to see two other women, be cool, relax, enjoy the ride. Don't blow it all by talking, you talk all the time, you talk to everyone and no one, you're the talker other talkers dream of being, but for once, just bathe in the perfection. Those legs, holy Christmas, no stockings.

You know that I know you, I know you know me, kitten, everything is here for us. I know that your senses tell you how alive I am, and I know you know I know women. We *both* know right now, which is the only time there is, all of the time in the world, I'm the only male riding on these rails who truly meets the standards of a man. Trou, yes, suits, commuters. Nimrods bedabbed with after-shave, men leading lives so tedious and gray they should be shot for the effrontery of breathing in our air, men who wouldn't know what to do with a woman if she came with an operating manual. They are commonplace but I'm unique. You know I know we both know I know what you want, and I will give it to you. You want me to notice you've been naughty. Very familiar with the type. Waiting for the headmaster to punish you. Slip those cotton panties off your rosy derriere, and spank you until your buttocks glow. Not *my* slice of heaven, ironically, but I give kittens what *their* hearts desire, anything at all to shed delight.

Rocking, rushing, racing on the rhythmic wheels of steel I stared in fascination as the past consumed the now. "Oh all right," mock gravitas, "I can't take it anymore. What is your name?" Diane, getting off in Baltimore, visiting her parents in Annapolis. No time we're discussing single-parenthood, dealing with a psychotic ex, human loyalty compared to canine, and the ten things we liked best about sex. Squeal of the brakes made us silent, already sad it would end. Phone number safe in my pocket, names of her kids, her address. Deal done sealed zaparoopie, kitten with a capital It. Opened up the kitten hall of fame for her alone, inducted her into the Puss Corps. Didn't have to call her, the seduction was complete, she would have done me right on the train. Knowing one can visit a Vermeer in the museum, in some respects is preferable to owning one.

Train got to the station, said goodbye to all the staff, knew every one of them by name. No matter where I found myself I had to work the room, trying out material, breaking in the act, making an impression everywhere I went. Always talked to somebody, frequently myself, if an audience was unavailable. Really got a charge out of being *overheard*, my objective was, of course, to be outrageous. When I hit Union Station it hit me right back. Recently restored to drop dead gorgeous splendor, turned out to the max for Christmas, sweeter than a millionaire's debutante daughter slowly sweeping down a spiral staircase. Felt as though I'd stepped into a new reality. Unemployed, close to broke, and facing the emotional demands of the season, forget about it, child's play. Don't think even Mick, big lip, Jagger strutting on the stage at the height of his career, ever felt more cocksure, cool, snozzy, handsome, or radnopolis.

There to pick me up, speaking of a millionaire's daughter, and I was, she was hypothetical and descending a spiral staircase when we left her, was Lilly. With Christmas carols ringing across the high arches of Union Station's grand hall, and I love Christmas music despite the commercial degradations it's subjected to, and Lilly, all five feet, ten inches of her wrapped in fur down to her ankles, things were perfect. Rather like a movie set. Suspiciously perfect. Almost too perfect. As if the entire situation with all the people and things had been put there specifically to mislead me. Felt like I was in a movie. I *was* in a movie. What a groovy movie at that. There was a bizarre extippitox sensation of hyper-reality. Not unreality. Had the feeling that I was an altered version of myself in a suddenly different world. As though, don't laugh, or do if you feel like it, aliens had scrambled my chromosomes while I was sleeping. Still had all the same parts but they were arranged differently. Had an enormously heightened sense of awareness, awareness of all things. All my senses were supercharged. Constantly restless, noticed everything. Endless streaming in of sensory data was snozzling, dizzying, sometimes overpowering. Look at those fabulous shops, gold trim over white, very royal French, tasty.

Lilly was a spoiled child, in plain English. In plane geometry she would be something else. I knew this instinctively all along but I'd been kidding myself that there was a future for us because she was so damned attractive and vital. Tall, black hair, green eyes, plain, open face, wonderfully animated. Always talking. Vivacious. Irresistible, girlish voice. Only in her mid-twenties and already making serious money. Hopelessly self-centered. Hard drinker, party animal, tease. For all that she was ravishing in fur, surrounded by Christmas carols and the bitterly cold wind. We got in her car. Our plan was to drive into Georgetown and have dinner, then hit the spots for some music. Lilly played the radio. I played hard to get, but it wasn't working. Perfect taste in music, jazz, soul, rhythm and blues that I liked. Uncanny really, the way her tastes in music matched mine, and mine were highly developed, highly refined. Music, (along with details, timing, a good profile, and having enough money in your wallet to leave town if you have to), it must be remembered, is everything. It's emotion. That Lilly *got* my music was an omen, a sign we were right for one another.

Rock star sensibility, chauffeured by a queen, music absolutely impeccable, reefer with a lot on its mind. Power window whined as I lowered it. Night air swirled bloody cold, *that's right*, he said bloody cold, knowing full well it was British English and sounded la-di-da from an American, loving it more for that reason, but it felt great. Toured me through D.C., could not believe it, street walkin' women everywhere. High-heel, hot pants, parade of prostitutes. Good God almighty, hot pants! Way below freezing out there. I'd already seen 42nd Street, the

French Quarter in New Orleans, even the boulevards of Rio, never saw anything that brazen before.

Dealers drifted in and out of shadows. After Lilly learned that they were interesting to me she pointed out the ones I overlooked, proudly showing off her knowledge of the city's outdoor theater of pain. Even found a drive-through crack mini-mart, cars backed up for a block. Could not believe the depravity, right out in the air. Of all of it the homelessness was hardest to absorb. Steam vents, lumpy blankets, death on the installment plan. Mad, alcoholic, helpless, each to his own disability. In the land of e pluribus unum, where guardians of the trust collected checks, where senators made billion-dollar phone calls, an almost invisible army stuck to the pavement like gum. Despite my lofty status I felt empathy. How could we allow this to happen, we who had so much? Nation of gluttonous waste and affluence. Dizzy-headed giddy from intoxicating rage. *No safety. No protection. Abandonment.* Chewed up by a cold and heartless government. *This* was what the world would do for those who couldn't make it. *Nothing!* Let them rot.

Lilly looked at me differently, almost as though we'd never met. After dinner we took in a club, but when we got back to my friend's house, she wouldn't even come in. Two of us hadn't made love yet, but we'd steamed up the windows a bit. Called the next day, whoops! She had plans. Did not make no kind of sense. Me being there was big. For months we'd been melting the telephone lines, now she had an engagement? Hot, pissed off, and furious. Told her that was it, I'd had it, really didn't need bullshit anymore. Told her she was losing the best man on two legs, the best man she'd ever know. Asked did she want to see me again, fish or cut bait situation. Lilly was demure, and she was never demure, *not the way you are right now*.

So Lilly never made it as a kitten, never joined the ranks of the Puss Corps. Oh what the hell, it was her loss, not good enough to make the cut. Suitable once perhaps, when my standards were lower, but not a likely companion for the meteor I was becoming. Called Hilary, singing to myself, *You don't want to crack up, get yourself a backup*. Hilary and I had seen each other a few times and she had a little crush on me. She was surprised, and thrilled, that I was in town. Was I *really* in D.C.? Took a cab to the restaurant where she worked. She was tickled, couldn't wait to get off. I couldn't wait to get off either, he said, unable to resist the cheap line, which wouldn't be the first time. Waited in the bar while she finished up. Snatches of a poem I'd forgotten, floated to the surface of my brain. You know how to make me sweat/Sometimes you're sweet/You're everything I haven't had yet/You're everything I want in a pet.

Drove me back to her place, townhouse in Alexandria she shared with two other women. By the time we got there the sexual tension was like perfume in the air, in fact I think it was, Eau You Kid. Hadn't seen each other for a couple of months. Got inside, mixed some drinks, went straight to her room. Never had been to her place before, when I saw it I busted out laughing. Looked like it belonged to a teenager, catastrophic clothing situation. Not a mess, more like a maelstrom. Clothes on the bed, the floor, hung from the corners of pictures, hardly a place to step. She had a huge, walk-in closet filled with clothes. I'd always known Hilary to dress exquisitely and now I understood it for the passion that it was.

"Hilary, my dear," broad smile, "I think you should clean up your room." Then, without a clue to where the notion came from, added, "for flavor, just to make it interesting, try them on for me, nice and tasty, before you put them away."

Relatively innocent at twenty-six years old, Hilary was game but inexperienced. Clever and excited, she caught on rapidly. After all, the rules were in her favor, all she had to do was get dressed and undressed, one of her favoritest activities. Only difference was, this time she'd be watched, every activity observed. Felt the blood roaring in my ears at the thought of what would happen next. Hilary *was* the girl for the job, built to electrify a runway. Tall, small breasted, svelte, firm and lovely bottom that gave way to a pair of exquisite legs as long as a sentence from Faulkner. Snatched up a handful of clothes from the bed and vanished into the closet, modestly closing the door as she did. Came out in an opulent silk kimono, long auburn hair around her shoulders.

"Delight me, Hilary," I instructed her, "pay close attention to the lingerie." She smiled, if she was scared, it didn't show.

Her arms had been folded, when she dropped them, the kimono parted wide enough to see she was divinely naked underneath. Smoothed on sheer silk stockings, clipped them to a garter belt. Shrugged her shoulders, ever so slightly, the kimono slipped to the floor.

"Is this what you had in mind?" she inquired. Play-acting coy, flirtatious, but, genuinely wanted to know.

"Yeah," could barely choke the word out. Then she picked up one of her brassieres, lacy and sweet as it could be, and adjusted it with sensual attention, until her girlish breasts were painted by its pattern.

She found a pair of black stiletto heels and put them on, gathered up more articles of clothing. Watched her every movement, mesmerized. She must have felt my gaze against her skin. Everywhere I went there were angels! She turned her back to me and from the perch of her high heels bent over to the floor and fetched some stockings. Stiff as a rake handle, buddy. Before we called it quits she'd been a dozen different beauties, statuesque in ball gowns with nothing underneath, cunning combinations of underwear, even some complete ensembles. She'd put her hair back up, and put it down again, half a dozen different ways, fiddled with necklaces and earrings, improved upon perfection with cosmetics. I was the mountin' man, she was the highest peek show, Everest about to climb Hilary.

When all of her clothes were neatly put away, we did, finally, make love. The heavy-mental foreplay had primed her to the point where she came almost instantly, thrashing back and forth like a tigress on the hunt, making sounds outside of my experience. Finished she descended into sleepy coziness, thanked me for my help with the room. Ushered instantly into the Puss Corps Hall of Fame, kitten with a capital *ten*. The satisfaction only fed my energy, dizzy jitters, wide-awake. Dreamy Hilary dreamt peacefully, all of her clothes put away, while I took care of business, feverishly, dusted, wiped, arranged, everything had to be precisely in its place, everything had to be just so. Finally the room was satisfactory, it looked as though a team of cleaning ladies had been working on the place for a week. Hilary had not noticed anything. I felt the breath of claustrophobia.

Dawn tracked me down at the station, by noon I was rocketing north. God only knows what she thought when she woke up, God only knows what she thought. Came home to the chaos only teenage girls create, woke up in Donna Reed's guest suite. Snat, rabazibby, magical man, magical wherever he goes.

Chapter 6

Rules Of Engagement

My mother was beautiful, smart, and good to her very soul. I early on got the idea that women were wonderful. When puberty hit, I jumped into the race like every other red-blooded American boy. I learned the rules of engagement in the battle of the sexes. I learned about coyness, flirtation, mixed signals. I fell in love with the intoxication of feeling that I'd found The One, The One who would answer all the questions. I fell in love with courtship, the distance from finding her interesting to getting her attention. Perhaps I was always more in love with romance than any individual woman.

But along the way, in high school and especially in college, I became a cliché. Not a happy fate for an insecure egotist. I became the kind of man you often hear women complaining about. "He does everything to attract you. He's nice, sensitive, says and does all the right things. He likes the things you do, walking in the park and holding hands, romantic movies, classical music. In bed he's tender and patient, as concerned with your pleasure as he is with his own. He's not like those brutes, those Neanderthals who never remove their boots and race down to the kitchen for Nacho chips and beer as soon as they've had their cheap thrill, leaving you alone with your frustration. He's a sensitive doll.

"You relent, cave in. You let him know you're falling in love with him. You press for a commitment, you want him to share his innermost thoughts. You want the boundaries between the two of you to melt like snow in spring. And then, poof."

The moment that happened, I was as gone as the age of steam. When pursuit became getting down to the real thing, I was nowhere to be found. I always explained it away as boredom, she wasn't interesting anymore, but that was a self-deception. The oldest saw in the basement, the dreariest ballad in the songbook, Fear Of Commitment.

I couldn't commit to anything. I couldn't commit to myself, much less another person. Clubs, political causes, religions. I watched and evaluated but I never had the nerve to jump in with both feet. I've discovered that loving somebody means risking it all, sharing it all, opening up completely. Back in those days I couldn't have spelled these notions. Dealing with the illness forced me to become that brave. If I hadn't had to cross that lonely desert, it might never have happened at all.

So I got on a merry-go-round, moving from one terrific woman to another. I always liked them, we were friends, I just didn't have the cheese to give them what they wanted. Attraction, romance, passion, flight, that was the pattern. And of course, it was always me who left.

Of all the women in my life, it was only my ex-wife who dumped me. She was nothing like my girlfriends. She was tough, critical, judgmental. Unforgiving. Always right, especially when she was wrong. I let her control me, perhaps I forced her to control me. Over time, my willingness to do that made her view me with contempt, and I began to resent her domineering nature. When she threw me out, she did me a favor. I say this from the sweet luxury of hindsight. Divorce shocked my system so badly that it drove my hair from dark brown to white practically overnight.

When the Mania struck, my genuine affection for women turned into something like cannibalism. Instead of being content with the attention of one, I had to have them all. If one didn't respond, there was always another one just around the corner. I had a limitless need for gratification and approval, like a really spoiled child. So it was natural that I'd go to women to fulfill it, after all, they'd given me so much happiness in the past. I liked them so much. And I found so much self-worth in being nice to them. But all the settings in my brain were horribly askew. I didn't think in terms of pleasing women so much as in terms of owning them. I behaved in a beastly way. I always hurt the one I loved, to the extent that I was capable of loving at all.

Chapter 7

Zelda

Back at home with a brain that boiled like a cauldron of Louisiana gumbo. What to, what to, what to do? Zelda bubbled up to the surface. Used to work together at an agency, still spoke now and again. Liked to feed me freelance. Didn't see her much, used the phone. Had always been a chemistry between us which I'd been very careful to discourage. Married chicks had always been off limits, police barricade, don't cross. And if that were not sufficiently sufficient, and it were, she was moody, spoiled, and unpredictable. Cheese not squarely on the cracker. But to quote the redoubtable Lord Buckley, "If you get to it, and you cannot do it, there you jolly well are, aren't you?" Which is another way of saying, I was looking at all career options, full-time freelance, free time full-lance, ad copywriting was a favorite. Half a dozen thoroughbred accounts in the barn and I could be completely independent. Fuck the corporate world and how they did me, wouldn't treat a stepchild like that, but like they always say, he who laughs last, laughs flaff flaff flaff flaff flaff. With projects pouring in from Zelda, and all the other angels I would meet, prosperity was unavoidable.

Called her, dropped my voice, picked it up again, began pouring rich, low, well-rounded tones into thin, brightly colored wires, triggering reactions in a distant living room. Anxious to see me, had a project, good one, too, something to get me through Christmas. Jackpot, snat, rapadoopy. Gonna' be fine, you bet. Getting laid off was serendipity, serendipity-doo. My oh my what a beautiful day. Reality forcing me into the light, success I'd avoided all my life. Tall, splashy, smashing Zelda asked me where we could meet, didn't know the city very well. Puzzled for part of a moment. Knew it had to be classy, only the best for her, smooth, elegant, easy to find. Time arrives in seasons, four points grip the globe, portents, clues, and omens, guiding me into a mystery. Didn't know where I was going, didn't even matter that I didn't know the way. The way knew me, and revealed itself. Zelda, resplendent at the Four, destiny decreed it, I obeyed. Gave her directions, gave her the time, four, four at the Four. Lately I'd become a fastidious dresser, meticulous and attentive, in the past I couldn't be bothered. Changed outfits repeatedly, room a wreck of clothes that wouldn't do, at last I got a look I liked to look at. Goddamn shoes, *horrible*, shine 'em up until you need shades. Details, accessories, by cracky, that was the battlefield. When everything else was kettledrum tight I tried on every tie I could find, especially the ones I wouldn't have touched just scant weeks ago. This was my new incarnation and it had to be sharp as attack. The smitten mirror stared like a schoolgirl, in the past it had avoided my gaze. Ready, so ready, big bad dog, big bad dog that I was.

Smoking a joint of the finest weed and purring towards the city in my spic and span sedan I was clean as an operating room. Took the scenic route through the park, cuddled the curves of the Schuylkill. Beautiful, gradually undulating, *that's right* he said undulating, calling to mind images of slithering snakes and belly dancers, road that allows drivers to watch crews rowing on the river, geese taking off and landing, an enormous variety of trees, and a great view of the city skyline. Made a point of being early, found a free parking spot on the street, nice trick in the city, entered the Four Seasons Hotel. From the white gloves the doorman was wearing down to the gleam on the brass, everything was perfection. Simply zapadoopy. Honey, I'm home. I'd been there before, but this was the new me and I was getting it fresh. There on business after all, my business. Into the lounge and sat at the tiny marble bar. Large room almost empty, clusters of couches and chairs. Soft jazz flowed from the piano, fountains murmured deferentially. There in that oasis was serenity and order, calm, and controlled posmondilism. In the past my instincts always drew me to the best but I saw that the best was a necessity. The new rule was that nothing but the best would be accepted, and only until something better came along.

Took a perch at the bar and soaked it in. Soaked it in what? Lemon juice? Why a perch? Why not a rainbow trout? My anxiousness level dropped several notches as I sipped a martini. Still no Zelda. Walked into the garden and smoked half a joint to nurse the perfectly mellow high along. Felt safe. Gonna' be chunky monkey. Business at the Four, write at home, visualized it taking shape. Reinventing myself. Once an idea was in my brain I could spin it out way into the future in seconds, watch it unfold like a movie. I had finally arrived. Then, Zelda arrived.

Zelda was ebullient in her full-length black mink coat. Late, of course, part of the charm. Big, put together, some would call her zaftig. Certainly not overweight, archetypically female. More scenic curves than Monte Carlo. Her ensemble was an artful interplay of business-crisp and pleasure-suggestive. Zelda, not a drinker, drained her cocktail down as if there was a prize at the bottom of the glass. Made short work of the project, raced headlong into gossip. What was up since I was laid off? What was I going to *do*? Said she was unhappy in her marriage. Zelda, never satisfied, restless hunger, intelligent, neurotic as a roomful of actors. Husband out of town *again*. Hint's a hint, wink's a wink, but when Zelda dropped that one I almost expected the *waiters* to turn their heads. Husband out of town. Looked like the kind of call girl that could mix gracefully at the White House. Friend, didn't know what to do.

Talk got more and more intense, eyes met frequently, girlish, giggly, flirting, but still a little coy. Finally asked her to dinner, sweet spot I'd discovered recently. Small, dark, romantic. Just signed off on a project. Iffy, but not *too* outrageous. Plenty of room to back out gracefully if either one of us got scared. Asked the bartender if he knew the number for the Warsaw Café, he volunteered to make the call. With every passing second I better understood how quality was measured in grace notes. I nodded. He asked if we'd like to be driven there, yes, of course, too good. Chauffeured, for free, in the hotel limousine, Zelda was thinking in mink. Feeling warm and cozy in the soft back seat. Comprehension materialized. This was how celebrities lived. Of course, it was me, a natural! What had taken so long? Balmy city evening, early in December, misty rain made everything soft, sweet, moist, tires pavement sizzled, purring in kitten cab heaven. Understood at last what my life was meant to be. Kittens waiting *for* me, kittens waiting *on* me, men providing menial service.

City scenery strained to delight us, holiday displays sought our approval, waitresses and waiters radiantly smiled, counting the colors in our halo. Zelda, long black hair, flicker candle flame, gypsy caravan long ago, far, far away, unknowable and irresistible. Wrong, wrong, wrong I told myself. The woman was married with kids. I knew if we did the deed our friendship would be over, an idea that did not appeal to me. I also knew a source of freelance work would be destroyed, *that* would be a catastrophe. Intellectual exercise, stacking mental blocks. Suddenly my mind went absolutely clear like the sky when a raging storm is spent. I understood how absolutely free I'd become, wanting and having were one. So she was married, so what? That was her problem, sure wasn't mine. She wanted me, I wanted her. In that idyllic visionary moment I felt the swell of grandeur in my soul, lightning in the tips of my fingers. Mores were for chowderheads and pipsqueaks. The appetites of great men were extravagant, society indulged them all the same. Culture offered endless examples, one could look at Mozart, Picasso. In fairness they were dead, they didn't look that great.

Truth, opportunity, and license fused like prongs on a fork. In the process of leaning forward while eating, Zelda had pulled her blouse partly out of her skirt, exposing a sliver of midriff, or was it a miver of slidriff? Held her gaze, slowly slipped a hand below the table. Touch sweet enough to open a safe, dragged a finger over her warm creamy skin. I was going on and on and on about some subject, my practice was to lecture all the time, seemed as though I'd recently become extremely clever, what I didn't know was not worth knowing. Zelda made no visible reaction but the sound sent a shiver up my spine. An utterance that hovered involuntarily somewhere in-between groan and gasp. Rules of gravity, rules of attraction, orbit dangerously compressed, collision had become inescapable. Decadent desserts, sweet waitress, *what now?* conversations on our lips.

Settled on the Barclay. Nearby, naparoopy. Classy old place on Rittenhouse Square next to the Curtis School of Music. Short walk from the restaurant. Plush quiet lounge, dark wood. Paintings, piano bar, rooms. Neither of us had said it yet but we knew it and we felt the tingling. Didn't want to drive all the way to my place, that would break the spell. This one had to be done right and it had to be done right away. We were adults about to do wrong, couldn't pretend we were kids. Guilt was for timid little people, the riches of the world go the brazen, shamelessness opens the oyster. WASPs, tediously tight, tied in knots of repression. Man breaks wind in elevator. Unfortunate, and yet, unavoidable. Remarkably the world doesn't end.

Outside in the clinging mist, slipped my hand in hers. Strolled the sidewalk leisurely, stretched the pleasure out. My normal pace had recently accelerated, just this side of a jog, felt to me like we were floating. Stopped and turned towards Zelda, reached into the coat. Eyes of a child, unequivocal smile. Pressed against her body, cloaked in luxury, kissed, and the kiss told a story. I'd known Zelda as a driven ad exec, kinetic, married with kids. Now I understood a different Zelda. Hot, hungry, female snozzler, craving snazzjungulation. Sped up and entered the Barclay.

Agitated by the proximity of so much guilty pleasure we sank into the leather of overstuffed chairs and danced around the issue that consumed us. I'd never played the married queen, hotel scene before. Much to my own amazement, I suggested a room. Eager breathy *yes* suggested she was crazy from waiting for me, but didn't make me feel like a bumbling amateur for taking so long to ask her. Such is the level of sensitivity women must perfect to navigate the shallow waters of the male ego's fragility. My credit card was able to absorb it, miracle enough on its own. Insisted on the best room available, something with a fabulous view. The elevator ride was one kiss long, Zelda pinned in a corner, free, furiously passionate. First swack happened in a flurry, can't imagine where the snow came from, but folks, as though our clothes had vanished magically. Tingling and relaxed, Zelda stretched on the bed, cat in a puddle of sunlight.

"I knew you'd be good, I just knew it." The smile she wore said *pleasure and fulfillment* like a chocolate mousse says, "I'm worth the calories."

Explosion number one out of the way we could chill and savor number two at a pace more civilized than bestial. Don't understand why so many men want to finish before they've begun. Why rush through something wonderful? The longer sex lasts, the more I like it. Packing a lunch seems reasonable. Unless it's because men find sex frightening and confusing and aren't interested in satisfying the women they love. Just a theory. Just a theory, that's a good one. Right up there with, just an expression. Just an expression indeed. Like, God is love, or, What goes around comes around? Just an expression! As though the phrases we use don't shape our thoughts and define our lives. Savoring a joint I looked her over, taking my own sweet time. Luscious, naked, voluptuous, grateful, satisfied.

"Tell me what you want, tell me anything. Tell me what a goddess dreams of doing."

"Own me, rule me, have your way with me, do anything you want." Zelda had a pair that beat three of a kind. Though not obsessed with breasts the way my culture seems to be, advertising illustrates the point, nonetheless I do understand their appeal. Rested my head on her bosom. Long crimson nails, carefully attended, painted earlier that day, scratched lovingly at my scalp.

"Zelda," nervous whisper, "do something special for me."

"What do you want me do?" she cooed, giggled, opened her eyes.

"Let me look at you in mink and lingerie," spizzled as I studied her response.

Silence, then finally, "God, you're so randy, I *love* it. I feel like I'm losing my mind." Statuesque Zelda stood, slipped on her panties, stockings, and bra, dove into slippery mink. Face up in bed as before, vision, charged, eroticism, nervous system meltdown.

Nice soft talk touch kiss caress. Feel of the fur on my hand, swell of her body beneath. Nipping me randomly, neck, shoulder, ear. Zelda's hunger, longing, she had dreamt of this, she had rocked herself to sleep picturing it all, now that she possessed it and it possessed her too she must have wondered what was real and what was just a dream? Zelda in her glory, thick lips curled up into an easy smile, wry laugh's incubator. Didn't own our bodies any longer, each had the other's to explore. Foreign was familiar, forbidden was allowed, mad with hedonism our pleasures multiplied, better than it could have been, better than imagined, better even still than how wonderful it was.

Which only fueled my appetite for even higher heights, everything good could be gooder. Making, taking, shaking, breaking love for who knew how long, started to interrogate her, *nothing* stopped my talking.

"Baby," I whispered in her ear, "what would you do for me?"

She wasn't really paying attention, and replied, eyes closed, casually. "Anything, anything, anything at all." The possibilities overwhelmed me, something too exciting to ignore.

"Would you do another man if I told you to?"

"Only if you picked him out for me."

"And would you let me watch the two of you?"

Big eyes opened suddenly, delighted, naughty smile danced across her lips. "*How could you be any hotter?* Yes, lover boy, you could watch us."

Had to go as far as I could take it. "Ever made it with a woman?"

Even in the darkness I could see her flashing teeth, grabbed onto me and laughed out loud. *"Oh dear God what will I do with you?"*

"Have you?"

"No."

"And if I asked you?"

"Yes my adorable maniac, I'd do anything for you. You could pick her out, you could watch us, God you are making me so horny." Zelda came, one of those bite the sheets orgasms with groans that began at the soles of her feet. I collapsed. My heart was banging louder than sneakers in a dryer. I lay down next to her. Hugged and entwined like ivy. She smiled. I kissed her and rubbed her body through the smooth, slippery fur, finally drifting to dreams.

When morning came we connected like magnets again, that one was for the bonus points. It was the randiest of all, especially because it was in broad daylight. We were both getting close to the border. Fortunately we had our passports with us. But folks. Quiet began as we finished. Suddenly it seemed like words cost twenty-five dollars apiece. We didn't analyze what had happened, or how things between us had changed. She switched gears into the girl thing. Shower, hair, make-up, the drill. I watched her getting dressed with interest, watching Hilary seemed like ancient history. Zelda's fabulous body, hidden from me, returned to modesty. Amazing how proper a woman can look regardless of what she's done. One fond farewell kiss was all. No need to say I'd be calling, had to, because of the job. Click, that was the end of it.

Stayed a little longer, smoked another joint, stared out of the window. Could see beyond South Philly, past the Navy yard, all the way to the airport. Looking at the city from God's point of view, down on the industrious people. Felt lonely. Had everything. Gorgeous women. Brilliant future. Power. Freedom to be whatever. I was King, it was unsettling. Played it over in my mind. I could have whatever I wanted. I was a star. Sittin' on top of the world, baby, days of mediocrity done. Ladies and gentlemen it gives me great pleasure to introduce the hardest working white man in show business, the world's funniest WASP, the only soul singer ever to emerge from Chestnut Hill, your favorite lounge lizard and mine, Alistair rhymes with Fred Astaire, Alistair McHarg. Rabazibby. Existing in memory only, gone, excused from the room, not here, no longer part of the equation, this cat's out the door.

Chapter 8

That Tiny Voice

That tiny voice. Everybody has one. That cricket on your shoulder that says, "No. Don't cheat on your income tax return. Don't lie about your weight. Don't vent your bad mood on your kids." Conscience, morality, ethics. Sometimes it's as simple as fear, guilt, and shame. Whatever you call it, it's the thread that holds the fabric of society together. Creates order. It gets in the way a lot, but without it, we're all sunk.

In my case, that little voice had a bullhorn. I grew up into the young man who wouldn't take yes for an answer. Well schooled and well educated, I could logically demonstrate the faults of anything and the futility of any act. If I'd ever gone to the trouble of having a motto tattooed on my shoulder it would have read, "Why bother?" I guess I believed that my dad had taken his share of success and my share too. So I opted out of the game altogether. You can't fail if you're not trying. Every time I did work up the nerve to step up to the plate and chance it, the tiny voice got loud. "Hey, you, where do you think you're going? Get your butt back on the bench where it belongs. You ain't big league material."

That little voice vanished when I was Manic. I existed in a moral vacuum. If I felt like doing something, I did it. If I wanted something, I grabbed it. I was immersed in the moment, with no thought at all about the consequences of my actions. Normally I'd consider all the possible effects of an act before making the first move. When I was Manic, I just didn't care.

My actions might have been reckless, cruel, self-indulgent, and ripe with bitter aftermath. Made no difference to me. All I felt was the passionate intensity of the moment. I was completely free from inhibitions, free from fear, free from constraints. A monster had been loosed upon the landscape.

Friends have asked, "When you were nuts, did you ever realize it?" There were times, when that tiny voice, this time without the aid of his bullhorn, tried to gain my attention. From the furthest recesses of my brain he would cup his hands and holler things like, "Yo, Al, baby, sweetheart, what in the name of Quick Draw McGraw is going on around here? This is not you. You never behave like this. Look at yourself and do something about it. Get help." But my brain wasn't moving a mile a minute, it was moving a mile a second. Every time I had a rational thought like that, my mind sent forty thousand angry thoughts after it to stomp it to death. The tiny voice didn't stand a chance.

As long as rational thoughts can be kept away, the illusions of the Mania can be sustained. I thought I was transcendentally brilliant, not mad. I continued to convince myself. But when that tiny voice came from the outside world, things became ugly. My ex-wife, my brother, when anyone tried to point my craziness out to me, the euphoria quickly turned to vehement denial. Anyone who stood in my path was shown the butt-end of my rage. My smoldering anger, normally buried deep and safely out of sight, was always just beneath the surface. No Manic can afford for someone to hold up a mirror. When that happens, the whole house of cards collapses.

And now a little secret. A tale told out of school. Something I share with everyone else who has my illness. I loved it. It felt great. I mean really great. Why else would so many Manics refuse to get treatment? They get hooked on their highs.

Can you remember the moment in your life when you felt the very best? Was it the day you got married? The day your first child was born? The day you scored the winning touchdown for your high school football team? Remember how you felt. Now double it. Keep going until the settings are turned up all the way to ten and your nervous system is buzzing like high voltage wires. Every pleasure center you have is glowing, you could burst into flames at any moment.

Now add a few more elements. You're incredibly strong, incredibly smart, and your energy is limitless. It gets better. You're totally without fear. That tiresome little voice, the nagging conscience, is dead. You don't care who you step on on the way up because you're not coming down. There's a separate set of rules for you, you're a Greek god, lightning explodes from your fingertips.

Of course it's all a horrible illusion, a lie of brain chemistry, adrenaline, body chemistry. But it doesn't feel like a lie. I'm sorry for how I behaved and I'm sorry for all it cost me. And I'm certain, certain, certain that I don't want to ever feel that way again. But my Lord, what a rare, profound experience. This life is short, and we don't get to sample all the things we would like. I'll never know what it feels like to hit a home run out of a major league ballpark. But. I know exactly how it feels to dwell upon Olympus.

And I know how it feels to be a Greek god rubbing shoulders with mere mortals.

Chapter 9

Shaky

Things weren't making sense. I was going on a sexual binge, doing things I normally wouldn't dare dream of, and getting away with it. As though the people around me were being swept up into the excitement of this new persona. Did I really have that much force of will? And if I did, then I could make anything happen. And if that was true, then I had something to be scared about. If there were no checks, no limits, no barriers I couldn't overcome, then I had some pretty scary power. That shook me the most. Not that events like joblessness would force my behavior, I was used to that, wasn't life a matter of reacting to undeniable demands? What rocked me was that my newfound strength of will, my power, would crush all that stood before it. If I couldn't control it, and others couldn't, what was left to protect me, and others, from me?

I went to the mailbox and emptied out the contents. I hadn't been home much lately and hadn't bothered collecting my mail when I was. Why should I? I had quite a bundle. I sorted through it at home. I had an impressive pile of bills, and no way of paying them. What little cash I had in the bank, and credit left on my cards, I'd need to live. There was no question of paying bills with that money. The money from Zelda's freelance job would be a month in coming. I tallied them up. Honeywell had given me two weeks' severance pay and paid me for some vacation time I hadn't used, so I'd gotten a small lump sum. But that was it. It was me against the sharks, and they all demanded their share. It was halfway through December and I hadn't even paid my rent. As I considered my situation, I started to sweat.

So I'm holding a stack of bills, sorting through them, writing up the totals, wondering what to do, when suddenly it hits me. Do the unthinkable. Break that taboo. Rules are for chuckleheads. Rachapootie. Just tough it out. The hell with it. Don't pay them. Sometimes they say of a fighter that he leads with his chin. Well, sure, you get banged up, but sometimes you have to lead with your balls. All guts. The world is full of people who get away with murder simply because they have the nerve to do it. I would be one of them. After all, I was poised for stardom. I didn't know exactly how I was going to get there but I was certain that outrageous success was just a couple of heartbeats away. Soon I wouldn't be concerned with money at all. The legal tender would be pouring in. I'd have a kitten to handle it. I'd just turn the checks over to her and she'd keep track of how much I was making. Hell, I wouldn't even carry money anymore, like royalty. Someone else would handle irksome details like that. Just put it on my account. Certainly, Mister McHarg.

It was an unorthodox solution, but then, these were unorthodox days. The point was to have the moxie. Satisfied, I started to pore over my pile of papers, a collection of things that interested me. The bills were on one side. Zelda's freelance job had an area. Business cards and cocktail napkins from my favorite restaurants and bars got an area. I started to spread things out, on the floor, on tables, tacked things to the wall. Papers, photographs, receipts. Artifacts. I was cataloging the elements of my life at the moment. The people, the places, the projects which would play roles in this amazing new life I was going to create. There were poems to write, rock bands to form, kittens to seduce, and what was I going to do about James Brown? He was in jail. I know there were reasons but how could the Godfather of Soul be in jail? Free James Brown. They made an example of him because he's a celebrity and because he's black. He doesn't belong in jail, he belongs in the Smithsonian. He's a national treasure. Good God. Rabazibby.

Chapter 10

Glitter

Being in the city had an advantage for me. City cops are jaded. There's constant action in a city. A car cruising at four in the morning doesn't raise an eyebrow. Try doing this in the lily-white suburbs sometime and see how far you get. There's very little traffic so the roads are easy to navigate. If you're floating on a raft of euphoria and marijuana, as I was, this can be very ooch rabazibby. And it's very otherworldly. Large, well-lit boulevards are deserted, as though a neutron bomb had been dropped and killed the people but left the buildings standing. Everything looks cleaner, clearer, more perfectly defined. It was just me and the cabs. The cabs, the cops, the hookers, the homeless, the dealers, the debris. It's a whole other world out there at night, a world of odds and ends, odds and unevens. Of things and people that don't fit nicely into proper categories. And I was snaking through it in the comfort of my mini-limo, high, warm, shimmying to the funky rhythms on the radio, pumped up on the power I exerted over my growing litter of kittens. I was bad. Bad enough to make it in the big time. Bad enough to rip the cover off.

So you cruise. Maybe put on the mirrored sunglasses for affect. Quite a bad affect when you're driving a black car and it's the middle of the night. Stop at a convenience store and get a pack of cigarettes and a cup of hot, black coffee. Survey the night crawlers, still can't get away from fishing, that hang out in these places.

Put your stuff on the counter and the clerk says, "Anything else?"

You say, "Yeah, I'd like a 'Free James Brown' poster and an eight by ten glossy color photograph of Catherine Daneuve taking a bath when she was fifteen years old."

The clerk looks at you with bemused boredom. "Two seventy-five," he says.

You look at your watch. "Holy shit," you reply, "I didn't realize it was that late." Before he gets a chance to tell you he's not interested you put down exact change. Exact change is wonderful. It means you don't have to wait and wait has become a major four letter word. Giving a clerk exact change is doing him a favor, making his job easier. Giving exact change earns a bonus point.

As you lay down the money you say, in a nice, conspiratorial stage whisper, "Keep the change."

By the time the guy's thought about it hard enough to *not* understand, which is quite a while in some cases since a lot of these guys rank just above squid on the evolutionary hierarchy, you're not Biology anymore, you're History. Maybe he gets it, in which case you've done a mini-set and provided someone with a laugh, a drop of delight. And I've seen delight. Maybe he doesn't get it in which case you've amused yourself, and at least you tried to break up some person's boring night with a little divinely inspired absurdity. In either case you've brought your art, your self, your being, into the now.

It was starting to get light. I thought briefly of another line from that old poem, Dawn is breaking/Dawn is breaking my heart. But it passed. Nothing stayed long enough to hurt. The thin winter sun was prying open the lips of the nocturnal clamshell. Everything was pink. I was feeling full of life. Juicy. Slurpy. Christmas was coming, less than two weeks away. I'd stay in town and search for the spirit of Christmas. Possibly even part with some money for presents. After all, I had a daughter who still believed in Santa Claus. She would be back in town with her mom soon, back from vacation, and spending Christmas with me. She had to have a perfect Christmas. I was recreating myself, my reality, my future, on an ongoing basis, nothing in my life was the same twice, but I certainly couldn't let a little thing like that prevent me from giving my daughter an ideal Christmas. Even in the midst of all this novelty there was something about a seven year old's belief in miracles, in Santa Claus, in the ultimate goodness of the unknown universe, that had to be preserved. But for me to be able to get into the task I would have to get myself into the Christmas spirit. This was my assignment for the day. Search for the spirit of Christmas, and infect myself with it.

I felt like walking so I parked my car in the lot next to 30th Street Station. Thirtieth Street Station is an enormous Greek style train station that stands next to an elaborate yard handling freight trains, local trains, and long distance passenger trains. It's a conduit for all North/South train travel. The station recalls a day when great power was based on rail transportation, before cars took over. But I'm not here to talk about what the station can recall, I'm talking about what I recall. It's a massive building with a main hall as large as a football field and a ceiling that's a hundred feet overhead. I remember as a child arriving in the station, climbing up the stairs from the train into the great hall, and feeling as though I was outside, the ceiling seemed that remote. On a whim I walked into the hall. There were early rising, upwardly mobile businesspeople swirling about, drinking coffee, reading the Wall Street Journal and licking boots just to keep in practice. Waiting for trains to New York and D.C. I looked up at the ceiling, puckered, and blew a note. It rang out in the hall, echoing off the marble, taking forever to decay.

Some things decay quite quickly, western civilization for example, but the note decayed slowly. I whistled the same note twice, two short blasts. Full bore, lots of volume, nicely amplified by the enormous hall. I drifted into a rousing rendition of "Ding, dong merrily on high." Walked around the room and tested the acoustics from different angles. People were starting to eye me curiously but hey, was that going to bother me? I found that it actually took so long for the sound to die that I could use the echo as a base and whistle on top of it. Now I was doing the carol as a round, using the echo as a second voice. I found this highly amusing, simply droll, just too too funny, trés amusante, and tried it out with several carols. God Rest Ye Merry Gentlemen. Good King Wenceslas. Joy to the World. The music intoxicated me. People were eyeing me suspiciously, as if to say, it's awfully early in the morning to be so cheerful, what's wrong with this picture? I Saw Three Ships. I was wailing now.

I kept walking around the room as I performed, harder to hit a moving target. I knew that sooner or later some long-suffering lowly hod carrier, some factotum, some dolt, some running dog lackey of the petite bourgeoisie would tell me to put a lid on it. Away In A Manger. To amuse myself I tried different tones and different speeds. With turbocharged intensity I whistled as fast as I could. Then I hit on something that gassed me. Boparoopie. The speed made it possible to hang notes in the air long enough to lay another melody on top of them. So I started whistling discordant pairs of carols.

First a phrase from Joy To The World. Then, with those notes floating above the heads of my unsuspecting and defenseless audience like angels with erections, (I should point out that it was the notes that bore a resemblance to angels with erections, not my audience, my audience bore a resemblance to alien zombies just back from a shopping trip to John Wanamaker's), a phrase from Good King Wenceslas. Back and forth. It took some puckering but I was getting such a jolt from it that I just kept going. An impromptu, improbable, Christmas happening in your face you whitebread corn pone brain dead blockhead. Something to tell your better half tonight. This guy, he was whistling two Christmas carols at the same time, it was weird. Rahsaan Roland Kirk, this is my Christmas present to you. A tribute to the immensity of your spirit. A little duty-free gift for the traveler. Roland Kirk, God rest his soul, should there be one, and if there is, fuck you pal, I'm tired of carrying water, do you hear me, was a wonderful jazz musician who, among other amazing feats too numerous to go into here, although I'm tempted, often played two saxophones at the same time.

When I hit the end of my number, lightheaded from the expenditure of breath, I headed for the door. I scanned the faces for responses. Some grins, mostly from the souls living closer to the cliffs. Some scowls. If they can't take a joke, throw them the hell off the bus. Some good old-fashioned confusion, what does it mean? But I felt good. I knew I'd nailed it to the wall. Alistair's extra-normal tribute to Christmas. Alistair, the man who plays flute, saxophone and train station. I hit the door without any slatch, no stationmaster's condemnation. A perfectly executed piece of performance art. Out the door he goes. Rabazibby. Striding into the gleam of a transcendental dream. Excused from the room. Existing only in your memory. Almost as if it never even happened.

I left the car where it was and started to walk towards city hall where the best department stores are. I would get the Christmas spirit by exposing myself to the throngs, the decorations, the music. I started to think about Christmas as I walked down the sidewalk at double speed, cruising in between the other pedestrians, weaving through the foot traffic like a runaway taxi, singing Christmas carols all the while. Excuse me, excuse me, excuse me, excuse me. Excuse me you dumb totally numb slave to the system excuse me. I'm light. I'm polite. What a thrill to be me. If I get too much better I should run for office. Tough day at the orifice, dear? People always looked, by now I expected them to. After all, I was a never ending performance, free to all, always changing. I was amazing. I meditated on Christmas. A celebration of God's son's birthday. A meaningful event if one believed in God. But this was tough. Could one really believe in God in a world which contained Barbara Streisand, Barry Manilow, Diana Ross, Spiro Agnew and Frank Sinatra? It asked a lot of one's suspension of disbelief. Do they build suspension bridges using suspensions of disbelief? Professional wrestling. Would God design humans so that their equipment for eliminating toxic waste and their equipment for lovemaking were right next to each other? And what about male nipples, was God careless and absentminded or did he have a bizarre sense of humor?

Apparently somebody needed to worry about these things and apparently the job fell to me. Hard to believe when I was so busy getting the Free James Brown movement going. I have to do everything, everything is my job. I wandered on. If God made the world, why was it that cockroaches seemed best equipped for it? And what about parking meters? Sometimes details are the most revealing. At this point it made little difference, Christmas was an enormous, tribal ritual barely connected with religion and I was involved with it willingly or unwillingly. I pressed on towards city hall, the focal point, the epicenter of Philadelphia. When I arrived there I saw a wild-eyed black woman with sandwich boards on either side of her which had scriptural quotes painted on them. She was wailing at the top of her voice, haranguing the passing Yuletide crowds, busy with their shopping. Hers was not a typical Christmas message.

"Demon dreamin' pimps of Satan worship calves of gold. But gold ain't gonna' help you none when God denies your soul," she screamed.

The blasé shoppers, accustomed to raving zealots as part of the urban landscape, were ignoring her. To me she was also a person and entitled to be treated like a person. And she was offending me beyond description as only a religious pontificator can, a person with the unmitigated gall to tell me what my religion should be. I slowed my runaway gait down to a normal pace and walked up to her. I stood right in front of her and smiled. She wailed on, every so often giving me the big eye.

"Excuse me," I said. No response. "Excuse me," I said again, "do you think you could tone it down a little bit? There are people here trying to use the sidewalk."

She looked at me but there was no glimmer of comprehension. I drew a deep breath and at the top of my lungs yelled at her, "Shut the fuck up. Shut the fuck up. Shut the fuck up." It washed off of her like rain, but I felt better. The shoppers close by looked at me oddly. I'd broken another taboo. You don't talk to a lunatic, you don't treat a lunatic like a person. She was troweling out this perverse bile but she was part of the scene. A person who looked like just another urban shopper slipping out

of character was far more bizarre it seemed. But I was furious
with her. She was pissing on my Christmas with her sickness. I
left her and entered Wanamakers.

Wanamaker's is the Philadelphia equivalent of Macy's, it's
the wonderful, grande dame of department stores. And it was
turned out for Christmas like the White House tree. In my state
of heightened sensual awareness, I was dazzled. Everything
glittered. Everything glowed. Nice Christmas music, not the
predigested kind, wafted off the marble walls. Everyone and
everything looked perfect. This phantasmagoria, this orgy of
Christmas opulence, this joyful pontippilance, had the look of
happiness. And what appealed to me most? Me, the guy who
had no money to shop for Christmas presents and had to use his
credit cards to live on? The skittish, prettiest kittens working
the counters of course. Young, adorable, dressed to perfection,
and best of all, captive so they couldn't escape my charm. I
worked the room with the single-mindedness of a panther. I
found the slishiest ones, flirted with them for a while, asked
them what they wanted for Christmas, always putting the focus
on them, which always worked because they were so tired of
straining in the attempt to satisfy others, and moved along.
No harm, no foul. They enjoyed it, which made me feel good
twice, once because I had done something nice for them, twice
because they had liked me.

When the bells rang signaling noon I decided to go to
the restaurant and have a martini. The bar at the restaurant
commanded a wonderful view of the gallery, an appropriately
princely vantage point thought I. Striding grandly by the
long line of tired, irritable, cranky holiday shoppers waiting
with only faintly concealed impatience to get in to eat, I went
straight for the bar. I had no thoughts of eating at all, I almost
never did. If I did find myself getting a little hungry I found that
a martini killed the desire. I spotted an empty seat at the bar,
amazing considering the horde, and claimed it. As I composed
myself, I discovered that I'd had the good fortune to sit next to
an extraordinarily beautiful woman. I ordered my martini. The
bartender was so light he had to put elephants in his pockets

to keep from floating up to the ceiling. If he'd been any more gay he would have broken out into song. Since I was the only man at the bar I was getting a lot of his attention. He started to fuss over me, insisting that it wasn't good to drink on an empty stomach. I should try the soup, it was wooooonderful. He had a point. I needed to eat, even if I didn't feel like it. I liked the idea that I was being cared for, worried about. Wait on me, I'm special. I had the soup and the martini, perfection. The woman was taking all this in without a comment. She was a Main Line princess from the jump. The kind of fashion model features that take generations of carefully selective breeding to achieve and a body as sleek and trim as a greyhound. She was in black from tip to toe with glorious blond hair and a perfectly appropriate smattering of gold accessories. If this girl, she was in her mid-twenties, had ever worked for anything, it didn't show. To the eye, she was faultless. Blemish-free. Unmarred. Peeled right off the pages of Vogue magazine. And mine. In one way or the other, she had to be one of my kittens. I knew that I would need a Mercedes outside, a house in town and another in the country, and a membership in the Philadelphia Cricket Club just to make it onto her "B" list. But that didn't mean we couldn't play Chinese Checkers. She held up a cigarette and I lit it for her, nobody has a faster lighter.

She said, "Thanks," softly. I asked her if she lived on the Main Line, she said, "Of course," as though it was obvious to all sighted people in the room. I asked her what she wanted for Christmas and she said, "Nothing."

How perfect, she has everything, more things would just be more things for the servants to dust. I asked her what her husband did for a living, a tired line that still worked, perhaps because it's just off center enough. She wasn't wearing a wedding ring so I assumed she was unmarried. "Please," she said, in a tone of voice positively dripping with fin de siecle ennui, I noticed this detail because there was a little puddle of fin de siecle ennui on the carpet, "I'm not here to meet anybody."

That's it kitten, bitch it out. Bitch it to the max. I know you and I know that you're at your very best when you're at your very bitchiest. I see you now with your idle class, silly, old school tie, topsider Maine vacationing boyfriends.

Standing tall. Naked, except for a gold chain around your firm tummy and a pair of knee-high leather boots.

Riding crop in your right hand, (because of course you ride kitty cat, I know that, the fox hunt, dressage at Devon, the whole fur-lined scene), your adorable puss pouting, fresh as a rose after a rainstorm, pink as spring lamb. You make them dress up in your underwear and lick the soles of your boots. If they clean the leather well enough, you reward them by wetting their thinning hair with your golden water. They adore you, these tedious madras clad boys masquerading as men. Then you allow them to take you to *Le Bec Fin* where you criticize the service. I know all this. No other man does. I scare you to death. I'm not like your vassals. Give me one Medieval weekend and I'd turn you into a wench, a courtesan, a strumpet. You sense the truth of it. Kitten, I love you. We both know the deal. We're brothers, sisters, soul-mates. In another lifetime we're doing the dance of desire so beautifully that the angels are applauding and the minstrels are writing ballads about us.

The martini was done, the soup was done, the waiter, who was watching this playlette like a soap opera, had a generous tip lying on the bar. I stood up and put on my coat. "Kitten," I said, "I'm not trying to pick you up." I buttoned my coat. "I've got more girls on my hands right now than I know what to do with." Now I had her attention. When you don't want them is when they want you. People are perverse. She turned directly towards me and looked me in the eye for the first time. Holy freakin' snozznopolis, I thought, she's gorgeous. I'm melting. These are the things that turn boys to men. Sunny days, everybody loves them, but tell me baby can you stand the rain? My God she was beautiful. "In your universe," I said, "you must make room for the possibility that there exists a man who likes you and doesn't want anything from you except the opportunity to praise your beauty, wish you a Merry Christmas, and disappear out of your life forever."

A little smile danced across her lips. Kittens wear mittens. And kittens are smitten. And being smitten can last a lifetime or it can last one beat of a butterfly wing. But it's being smitten all the same. Oh fellas, if I could teach you how to do this I'd be the richest white man in Christendom. And nothing feels better. In her mind she was laying down as smooth and easy as two-lane asphalt on a summer afternoon. In a completely unguarded tone she whispered, "Thank you." I held out my hand as if to shake hers, to seal our pact. With impeccable manners she unchilled her reserve for a moment and held out her hand to shake mine. I touched her hand softly, looked her in the eye, winked, and kissed it as lightly as any Elizabethan prince would have. The bartender gasped. She shivered, just a quick little quiver racing up her spine. I turned. Out the door he goes. Rabazibby. Almost as if it never even happened. Once you've been touched, you're changed forever. Existing only in your memory. Try to forget me princess, try all you like. While your boyfriends drive you in their Jaguars, you'll be dreaming that I'm driving you out of your mind.

Chapter 11

Claire

Reinstalled as the Prince of the City, I left Wanamaker's and headed east on Chestnut Street to continue my search for the spirit of Christmas. It was now a glorious, brutally cold, winter's afternoon. In no time I was down by Independence Hall, one of my favorite buildings in the world. It looked every bit as beautiful as it could on any idealized post card. I studied it and laughed. If anyone was paying homage to the dream that began there over two hundred years ago it was me. Never had a man been so free, and so ready to assume a new and powerful destiny. I was still uncertain about what I was to become but I knew it would be unimaginably grand. After all, wasn't I making an impact everywhere I went? Hadn't I discovered an astonishing source of energy? Wasn't I bubbling with observations, insights, revelations? It seemed inevitable that soon I'd be discovered by some entrepreneurial soul who appreciated just how doggoned amazing I was. And then, well, the rest would just fall into place. Money, television appearances, women, limousines, travel to exotic hot spots, I saw it unfurling before my eyes like a foregone conclusion.

I wandered into the Bourse, a stately Baroque building bordering Independence Square, recently restored to its original splendor and lined with exclusive shops. Like John Wanamaker's it was divinely dressed in its Christmas best. My astoundingly good instincts once again had led me, without any thought, to the right place. A boy's choir was performing Christmas carols.

While they may have lacked the originality of my train station performance, their presentation was professional and heartfelt. It reminded me of my days in the boy's choir, where I got my first musical training. That was a sweet, idyllic recollection which did wonders towards putting me in a Christmas frame of mind. On the main floor an arts fair had been set up, to take advantage of the Christmas buying fever. I started to walk through the various displays, mostly the usual stuff, jewelry, pottery, photographs of scenes so unashamedly sentimental that Norman Rockwell would have been embarrassed to paint them. I was singing as I went, I'm always singing. But I was off my Christmas track for the moment. The recollection of my boyhood days as a chorister had made me melancholic, an emotion I associate with Christmas, and I'd launched into a Jimi Hendrix ballad that has always haunted me, *The Wind Cries Mary*. I'd strapped on my heavy duty, radio announcer voice to match the pathos of the song and was well into it, doing a pretty nice Jimi Hendrix impression even if I do say so myself, and I do, because if there's one thing I do almost too well it's sing like Jimi Hendrix, which is important, since he's not around to do it any longer, when I turned the corner of one of the displays and was stopped completely cold by a group of paintings.

Being stopped by something utterly befuddled me, me, the guy who knew everything regular folks knew as well as things that nobody else knew. The paintings were exhibited in a booth which was being supervised by a woman who was reading. The first one I noticed showed two large red hands, coming from opposite ends of the canvas, the fingers almost touching. One hand was coming down so that the wrist was in the upper left hand corner and the fingers were in the center, the other hand was coming up from the bottom right hand corner, fingers in the center. The hands were very close to touching, tantalizingly close. The execution of the hands was wonderful but what really undid me was the title, "Trapeze Tragedy." I stopped walking, stopped singing, stopped fidgeting, stopped thinking about how to get James Brown out of jail, and for a moment just laughed. The tables had been turned. It was always me cracking other people up, me performing, me controlling the responses. But this just undid me. It was too funny, too unexpected, and frankly, much too very very. I looked at another. It was done in exaggerated cartoon fashion, a la Lichtenstien, with big, brightly colored dots resembling enlarged print impressions. It showed a murder scene. A corpse lay on the floor, its face horribly contorted into a terrified grimace. A policeman stooped over the body while another policeman took a photograph. In the foreground of the picture the coroner was filling in a death certificate. In the line next to the words, "Cause Of Death," he'd written in, "Compliments." When I saw this one I really broke up, I laughed as hard as an unhinged hyena. "This stuff is wonderful," I said. I looked at the woman. "Did you do it?" She just smiled and nodded.

I looked at another, it was a trompe l'oeil of a needlepoint sampler, one of those things which usually have a boring homily like There's No Place Like Home sewn onto fabric along with some simple illustrations like houses or maybe the alphabet. But instead of a bromide this sampler said, "I can handle the despair, it's the hope I can't stand." I just was not ready for this stuff. It was nuts. It was unexpected. It had a squizzling kind of snerchiness to it. "I heard you singing," the woman said. "It sounded good." We fell into talking as I looked at the other paintings. Her name was Claire. She was striking, I could tell by the placard in her hand, but folks, medium height with jet black hair. Not a princess like the kitten at John Wannamaker's but still, there was something about her. Something naparoopie, and yet, with just an added suggestion of crocodiles sunning themselves on the banks of the river Nile.

Cue Sun Ra. Sailboats, on the river, the beautiful river, on the river Nile.

We connected immediately. As though we were on the same wavelength. A permanent wavelength. If reality is when two people share the same dream, maybe I'd found the person to share mine with. Pretty girls, even with inflation, are a dime a dozen. But an artist, with a divinely inspired sense of humor, who liked my singing, well, this could be it. There's no protection against love, even a Lizard King can be undone. And isn't it always the one you wouldn't expect that manages to get under your skin? And why am I asking you? I found out from her that the show would be there one more day and that she'd be there too. I took a business card. I had to get going, I was getting restless, Christ I'd been standing still forever. I knew I'd be back the next day.

Chapter 12

As Unaccustomed As I Am To Public Speaking

As unaccustomed as I am to public speaking. When Harpo Marx went on the after-dinner speaker circuit, he would frequently open up with this line. It got roars. With a first line like that, he really didn't need a second line.

The truth of it is, the likelihood of me performing for an audience is about as great as the likelihood of Harpo Marx opening up his mouth and speaking in a Marx Brothers movie. His basic shtick was that he never made a peep. And so was mine.

I have spent a lifetime avoiding the spotlight as though it were a death ray. They say that one of the most basic human fears is public speaking. Perhaps mine is no more pronounced than average. But it feels like it is. I can withstand anything but large doses of attention. I can endure anything but approval. I'm brave enough for anything but the judgment of a thousand critical eyes, all trained on me.

The closest I ever came to leaping over this pit of fear was in college when I was the lead singer in a rock band. I suppose that my desire to be cool overwhelmed my fear of making a fool of myself. We were pretty good and we played a lot of dates. But that dread of planting my heels and facing the crowd was monumental.

Who was I to demand their attention? Why on earth did I think I was good enough? What would I do when that one small child pointed out that the Emperor had no clothes? I was so shattered that I literally shook. I used a very old remedy. I drank booze to steady my nerves. When I got beyond the nervousness and just had fun with the music, it was great. But that first step!

I do very well one-on-one and in small groups. I'm a natural entertainer, always a joke up my sleeve and a song in my head. I'm a natural teacher as well, very professorial. I love to share what it has taken me so much work to learn. In truth, I crave attention. But approval embarrasses me. Praise makes me suspicious and leaves me at a loss for words.

I find delight in entertaining people. It's as simple as the pleasure I get from making people happy. But try taking these skills into a room with over twenty or so and I'm dead. I hope to kill this fear one day, but I haven't yet. Perhaps I'm still not ready to say I deserve the attention.

That's what makes my Manic behavior so amazing. Whistling in the train station. Comedy performances in convenience stores. Belting out ballads in the middle of art shows. Wildly inappropriate. Bombastic. Grandiose. Magnificently fearless. Not just facing an existing audience. Creating an audience. Commanding the attention of an audience. And commanding it with something far outside the mainstream.

This was a level of courage and showiness I'd never imagined and never wanted. Of course it wasn't truly courage because it was involuntary. It just happened. I had no idea what I was going to do from one moment to the next.

But I have to stop before I beat it up too badly. There's an element of pure joy, pure creativity, and pure freedom in all of this. Some of the behavior is abysmal of course, but some of it is fun, funny, and innocent. Amazing things happen when the mind is released from its fetters. Wild combinations of things, bizarre new creations. Some are good.

I had fun, big fun, blowing those notes in the train station. It felt great, it was hilarious, and even though I was sweating and mad, I was nothing less than delighted with myself. I was celebrating myself with a grandeur that Walt Whitman would have envied.

If only I could learn to do that in real life, and turn down the volume just a bit.

And why did the illness hurl me into the spotlight, the place I dreaded most? Was that just coincidence? Or was there a secret part of me that saw the opportunity of a lifetime? The chance to feel what it was like to be a celebrity. A star. I don't know. Perhaps my heart of hearts desperately wants that celebrity, but that terrifying desire is safely locked away. So far away that I'm not even aware of it. And then, when the Mania took over, every strange hunger was fed.

Chapter 13

Steps

How wonderful life is when you've dropped out of the mainstream. You shop when there's nobody else in the stores. You drive when there's nobody else on the road. Everything is more convenient. It was dusk. The sweet darkness was falling on the landscape like snow. I was heading into town while everyone else was heading out. They growled, inching along, individual cells in an enormous mechanical snake of cars, winding along the river. I was gliding along with barely another car to contend with. Refreshed, rested, meticulously dressed, puffing on a marijuana cigarette, right arm resting on the top of the passenger's seat, I had the swagger of Rasputin mixed with the nonchalance of Fred Astaire. Prince of the City. Master of the Puss Corps. So much to discover. I could be anything to anyone. What do you need to know, I can tell you. The strangest thing of all was, I had been this amazing, charismatic monster all along and just didn't realize it. It took being thrown out of the corporate mainstream to discover the extraordinary powers I had. To the tune of Native New Yorker I was singing, You should know the score by now, you're a monitor lizard. A monitor lizard with pretensions to the title of Komodo Dragon.

I returned to the Bourse and found Claire, again seated, reading, surrounded by her fascinating work. I looked at a large painting I hadn't noticed before. It was a close-up of a bicep with a tattoo which said, Art—Craft With An Attitude.

There was another one next to it that had a huge black dot on a white background. It was titled, "Art is the shortest distance between two points, one of which has no known location." I was knocked out by her stuff all over again. I picked myself up off the floor and waited for the next round to begin. We began our conversation where we'd left off. No matter how offbeat my references were, she seemed to stay with me. Was she as brilliant as me? Another visionary? Another truth teller who'd had the blindfold removed? It seemed impossible, but wherever I went, she went along too. I kept looking into her eyes, she never flinched. A companion for my new incarnation. The others were kittens, playthings, snozzlers, but this was an equal. Someone who could keep up with me. Someone who knew the difference between rabazibby and naparoochie, and it's amazing just how many people don't. I was stunned. She closed up her booth. With no awkwardness at all we decided to go have a drink. There was a marvelous place in the Bourse, Oggi's of Paris. Very chichi. Lots of mirrors, elaborately arranged fresh flowers, high fashion, steps to various levels, polished chrome. Said to be a favorite haunt of the South Philadelphia Mafiosi. When we got inside I immediately felt more comfortable. Having recently been there I already knew the entire staff by name. My ability to remember names was astounding. Add that to my ever-increasing list of abilities which proved beyond debate my superiority to the horde. The herd. The common people. But don't misunderstand. Noblesse oblige isn't all bad. Like any true prince I loved the common folk and deeply felt my obligation to their welfare.

Claire looked less comfortable. Her mode of dress was peasant under glass. Jeans. AHH. Jeans, the fashion cliché of the century. Let's banish jeans back to Colorado to adorn the butts of cowboys should there be any left. But still, I wasn't going to fault her for a little thing like that. She had on a nice sweater with swirls of purple, pink, and blue, over a black turtleneck. Massive, silver earrings. After we'd been talking for a while I realized that one of the earrings had Yes stamped through it and the other one said No. While I was uncertain about what my new identity would be I was absolutely certain that it would be out of the mainstream. Jazz singer. Poet. Performance artist. Snozzledrostopist. Collage creator. Talk show personality. It made perfect sense that a woman like this was right for me. A woman who understood the artistic mind. A woman with whom I could share my extraordinary, unorthodox adventure. A Eulipian. The universe had sent me my little reptilette, the lucky girl who was going to share in the incredible bounty I was about to reap. So. Get it? I was smitten, swooning at the thought that I might not be taking this fabulous journey alone. Really happy. All the evidence was there. Amazing how things were falling into place for me. The less I tried, the better things worked out. As though I was being directed, prompted. As though my life was controlling me, and I was just tagging along for the fantastic ride. As though I was serving a higher calling, something I didn't understand. All I had to do was be careful to read the signs, stay alert, and the harvest was all mine.

I asked her if I could walk her to her car. To my surprised delight, she'd taken the trolley, since parking was so impossible. I offered her a ride home and she accepted. This was going like clockwork, I thought, pinch me. Ouch. We walked to my car. There was a parking ticket on it which I tore in half and carefully deposited in a trash can. One simply doesn't litter, unless one is a kitten. Littering is Not U. We began our drive. It was starting to rain a miserable, cold, sleety rain which, had it had any self respect at all, would have been snow. She started to give me directions to her house. I knew the area, West Philadelphia. A North East equivalent of Beirut. Past 30th Street Station, past Drexel University, past the University of Pennsylvania, across 40th street where the panorama turns very black very quickly and the income level drops like a spent roman candle. I'd lived out that way briefly, years before. A very dangerous neighborhood indeed. Home of the infamous MOVE tragedy, when the city government actually bombed a house containing some black, radical anti-social types and burned them like so much barbecue chicken. Instead of trying to put the fire out, the firemen watched as an entire block went up in flames. Not that the termination of the MOVE desperados was any great loss mind you. You see, telling the truth goes beyond political correctness, beyond being liberal, beyond being sensitive. Telling the truth means that everybody hates you.

When I let go of society I gained the power. Even T.S. Eliot, that bloodless sack of shit, said humankind cannot stand very much reality. Well I've got reality on sale, kids, how much would you like today? Would you like small or large fries with that? Not a neighborhood for faint hearts or cream puff liberal white boys from the suburbs but then, the universe was sending me here and who was I to argue with fate? Radical, ultra-liberal whites, low income to no income blacks, lunatics, homosexuals, drug dealers, crack addicts, extippitox slatch-heads, alcoholics, Koreans, Vietnamese, thieves, musicians, homeless, latchkey children, expatriates, political revolutionaries, college professors, and Claire's house. The cliffs. From here I could see infinity, no bourgeois material trinkets to distract me. But I'd better not slip up. Like the mighty Laura Nyro said, they hang the alley cats on Gibson Street.

She showed me her house and I found a parking place in front of a Cadillac with four flat tires. I looked at the house. The only thing missing was thunder and lightning. I fully expected werewolves to start howling in the distance. It was quite typical for the neighborhood. Three stories. In the naked city. But folks. Gothic. Stone. Perhaps a hundred and twenty years old. Elaborate ironwork over all the windows and doors. Large porch. Completely dark. An abandoned building next to it was in an advanced state of decomposition, more like ruins than a house. It was the kind of neighborhood where even the trees didn't look natural. Quite simply I knew then and there that I was entering another world. This house was going to be mine. This would be my world headquarters. This would be where I returned after my rave review round the world rock tours. Ladies and gentlemen, please welcome Alistair's All Reptile Review. This would be the castle where I kept my kittens. This would be where the art would happen. There was magic here, snozzling of a sort almost completely unknown in this part of the world, this was a place of madness, of divinity, a clean slate for me to write on.

Claire and I got out of the car. I locked it very carefully. We climbed the steps up to the porch. It was cold as death and I wanted to get inside. Claire was unlocking the door, a procedure which involved padlocks, several keys, deadbolts, creaky hinges and a lot of time. I was crazy for her but this was working on my patience. At last she got the door open. After passing through a vestibule we walked into a massive front living room. It was lit by one, large candle and was cluttered by what looked like African musical instruments. An enormous black man in African garb and long dreadlocks was sitting on the floor across from a white woman also on the floor. Her hair was either filthy and matted or else strangely assembled in a bizarre imitation of dreadlocks, or both. They were chanting. Claire beckoned me past them towards the kitchen, they ignored us entirely. "That's Prince Wilson and Ultraviolet," she said when we'd made it into the kitchen. "I would have told you about them before but I thought I'd let you discover them in your own way. They live here too, I rent the second floor to them and I live on the third floor." I was just knocked out altogether. Obviously I'd been in the suburbs much too long. This menagerie was a revelation. Claire and I sat and drank wine in the kitchen as our conversation twisted and turned in the air like a plume of smoke. When it came time to say goodnight I didn't even try to go upstairs with her. It was special. It had to be handled with care. She let me out the front door, even that procedure required several keys. If you didn't have the keys, you couldn't leave. It was strange, being let out like that, almost like prison, but I didn't think about it much. I was enchanted by Claire. She'd put a spell on me. We shared a quick and innocent goodnight kiss, I told her I would call, and meant it, and she started once again the elaborate machinations of securing the door.

Now, back in the freezing rain, I heard a police siren wailing somewhere nearby. The sound came closer and threw the neighborhood dogs into a frenzy. I moved quickly into the security of my car. I dried my face and arranged myself for the trip, letting the car warm up, looking at Claire's house. I'm a traveler. I go to places that others would be frightened to dream about. I'm cut loose. Now I dance through the world with laughable ease, seeing everything, while others struggle with their blindness. I'm a voyager. I'm among you, but I'm not one of you anymore. I pulled away slowly and the tires started to hiss on the wet, slippery pavement. The biggest reptile in the city started to slither home. No traffic now either. When you drop out of the mainstream, everything becomes easier.

Chapter 14

The Righteous Rage That Drives Men Into Battle

My father used to speak of something called a "Celtic rage." It was a sort of fit, a blast of furious energy responsible for winning many a battle in the Scottish Highlands. I've always felt connected to those mountains, those ancient times. Those wild, fierce souls. The sound of bagpipes gives me the chills. Each time I visit the Highlands I wonder why I don't live there, I feel such a sense of belonging. I look like I'm from Scotland. I have that same lonely independence. That dour, I'll suffer anything mentality. And I certainly have that same Celtic rage coursing through my veins.

My father used to lecture almost constantly, and his stage presence was remarkable. Time after time he would rail against the degradation of the environment. Then he would identify the culprits. Big business. Short-sighted, greedy developers. He was especially fond of recommending ritual disembowelment for all members of the Army Corps of Engineers. No invective was too cruel, no statement too outrageous.

As he built up to a full head of steam, his Scottish brogue unfurled and his mustache bristling, he began to resemble a possessed fundamentalist preacher. He spoke of this hideous destruction with breathtaking, self-righteous, moral outrage. There was no mistaking his certitude. He knew he was right. He was furious. He knew who the guilty parties were and he knew why they did it. It worked. People loved it. It was great show business. But it was scary. It had the look of madness.

What, in fact, was he really so angry about? What, in fact, was I so angry about? When I was Manic I smoldered with a sense of righteous indignation, furiously defending the undefended. Was I really just defending me, without knowing it? As with everything else, having my anger on the surface like that was a unique creation of the illness. Normally I could go for a decade without losing my temper, I was wrapped that tight. The child of European parents, I was so well-mannered that it was almost a problem. Friends told me to loosen up, relax, do something spontaneous. Expressing anger, even having angry thoughts, these activities simply weren't in my emotional portfolio. On those rare instances when I did express anger, it was expressed self-destructively, so that I wouldn't hurt anyone else.

Consciously, of course, the Manic me thought I was on top of the world. But in the real emotional household, far from the out-of- control brain, I was so, so hurt. Most of all I was hurt because I'd played by the rules and been a good person and it hadn't made a damn bit of difference. I'd struggled so hard on my own, gradually reconstructing my life after the divorce and the first Manic episode. I'd been a good father, really loving and responsible when it wasn't easy, and it hadn't made a damn bit of difference. One wave of the layoff wand and it all went away, including my sanity.

Of course if you dug a little deeper there was plenty I was hurt and angry about. I was really torn up about what had happened to my marriage. I was brutally hurt, and angry with the kind of anger that makes you shake your fists and scream at the Gods, by my mother's horrible death. My father's preoccupation with himself was another source of anger. It really bit me. It bit me because it made me feel small and unimportant.

That seems like enough, but it goes even deeper than that. Some anger, some pain, comes right from the center of my soul. Some of this I was born with. I'm rarely aware of it, I almost never express it. I am, perhaps, afraid of it in the same way that

I'm afraid of assuming the power which I have and which I shamefully squander in my stupid excuse for a job. It's far too deep to have been entirely learned. Call it Celtic Rage. Call it a holy fire of fierce intolerance, contempt for evil, disdain for stupidity. Call it what you want, but beware of provoking it.

That anger, which had been living in a wet, dark dungeon most of my life, had a field day when I was Manic. Though I felt like I was riding high, real viciousness was never far away. Even my jokes, though I thought they were funny, had a razor's edge to them. I was more anxious to make people squirm than make them feel good. It was payback time, and I had a whole lot of venting to do. The Mania transformed me into a bizarre reincarnation of my father. I had the furious fire.

Chapter 15

Christ

Back at home, switched on. Can't sleep. Zazazazazaza. Middle of the night. Claire on my mind. Soon Paula and her mom would be back from vacation and I'd have to be together. Got to stay together when I have Paula and she would be with me for Christmas. Got to get myself into a nice, Christmas frame of mind. Understand Christmas. Understand the real Christmas. I put on the best, purest Christmas music I could find, closed my eyes, and thought about Christmas.

Well let's see to begin with Christ was a soul brother so all the black hating so called Christians can get off the fucking bus at the next stop look at the part of the world he was from who the hell do they think he looked like, Basil Rathbone? Lawrence freakin' Olivier? Leslie be a good fellow and pass the bleedin' Rothmans Howard? Why can't they get with the program he was olive skinned to begin with at the very least and spent most of his life outdoors soaking up the desert sun. How irritating when reality refuses to conform to prejudice.

And of course Christ was a Jew, Christians are people who believe in the teachings of Christ, Christ, however, was of the Jewish persuasion, why am I the only person willing to point this out? So that means that all the anti-Semites are also invited to remove their misbegotten bottoms from the fucking bus. A person cannot be anti-Semitic and be a Christian at the same time, this is a square circle, a thing which cannot be, by definition. My mind understands great truths, truths which others either cannot see or refuse to see. My mind has all the answers, is there anything you need to know?

Can you understand the painful weight of being wise when all of those around you are blind?

The Christ of the Bible would have been offended, not to say nauseated, nauseated, there I've said it anyway, by the way we celebrate his birth, an orgy of meaningless gift exchange. He would recommend something less difficult, like buying dinner for a homeless person, or spending an evening reading to someone dying of AIDS.

We spend one day a year celebrating the birth of Christ, the other three hundred sixty four we spend celebrating the birth of Satan.

When Christ was born, he was in stable condition.

According to the best scientific evidence available Christ was born in the summer we celebrate his birth in the winter because early Christians hoping to increase their popularity through the use of clever marketing co-opted existing pagan rituals focused around surviving through the cold to see another spring boy did it work.

The Jews did not kill Christ imagine being punished for two thousand years for a crime you didn't commit the Romans killed Christ to make things worse as if killing Christ wasn't bad enough they didn't even want to shrewd politicians that they were they knew a martyr was more difficult to defuse than a live hero Christ practically forced them into it.

Ah the tender charm of Christmas carols.

Zealots roasting in an open fire

The Inquisitor is tearing off a nose

Holiday songs being sung by a choir

And soldiers are gambling for your clothes

Everybody knows

That's one you won't be hearing on the top forty real soon that's the kind of music you can only hear on my radio station WART all reptile music all the time with no commercial interruptions.

Let's put the Christ back in Christmas and the Hgghhgg back in Chanukah.

One small candle can start a fire to light the heavens there are many doors into the temple it doesn't matter which one you enter everyone knows it but they're just afraid to say it I know that everything I say is brilliant but sometimes I just don't know why yet we celebrate His birthday now because it's a gloomy time of year and we need to reaffirm the spirit of life of hope but he's gone real gone solid gone out the door rabazibby gone checked out no forwarding address gone never to return gone and whosoever really loves Christ and wants to find him to honor him to rejoice in him shouldn't look under a tree they should go to a prison a loony bin a ghetto a hospice or just get onto the streets and look under the blankets there by the steam vents forgetting about buying things giving things away instead to people they don't know better still not give things away give self away as He did finding the people nobody else wants the cripples the lepers the debauched degraded decadent sinners because Christmas and money are oil and water the more people spend the less they know about Christmas God assuming there is one sent us his Son He didn't send us a set of toy trains let's just change the name to Giftmas and drop the pretension altogether or get with the program get real roll up our sleeves and get on with the deal.

Let's be brave grown up puppies and kittens and admit the horrible truth God didn't make Man in his own image Man made God in his own image it makes so much more sense it explains so much God's not real man's *hunger* for God is real because without the conceit of believing in a God who makes sense the world is actually the chaotic cruel place it seems to be the unjust place where kindness is punished and cruelty is rewarded a place where virtue really is its own reward its lowly reward its only reward.

Let's expose heaven for what it actually is the greatest marketing gimmick of all time the perfectly unsubstantiatable claim can anyone prove it doesn't exist well there you are.

It goes like this. One priest is talking to another.

"We'll take these ignorant peasants and convince them there's a heaven. That'll give them something to dream about. But, we'll tell them that they'll never get there if they don't obey all the laws we give them. We can make the rules as fuckin' goofy as we like. It's gonna be great. We can restrict their diet. Tell them whom to marry. Here's a good one, we'll get 'em to mutilate their peckers with rusty knives! And of course, we can get them to give us their money! We'll make them recite really wacky prayers and stand up and kneel down a lot. We'll give them a lot of shit to memorize. We'll convince them that they're dirt if they don't listen to us. And, here's the best part, we'll convince them that they're born guilty so they've got no chance of getting to heaven if they don't do what we tell them."

Sometimes the most insane ideas work the best.

An idea which is just slightly off is easy to spot but a completely insane idea can be presented as just too brilliant for conventional minds to fathom and people bought this promotion in a big way religion is the con that controls the masses the ultimate false promise we could have heaven on earth today if that's what we wanted it isn't more people have been slaughtered in the name of religion than saved when you're totally bankrupt morally and without any authority is when you're most likely to claim God's endorsement who can prove that you're wrong if we were less sold on the idea of heaven maybe we'd work a little harder to be moral in this life ah but then we'd be harder to control we'd demand more of our leaders we wouldn't stand for the shameful way we treat each other.

In heaven, are there neighbors to look down on? Does God give lectures once a week? Can you screw up and get thrown out? Do you have to act serious when God is talking? Is there humor in heaven and if so, at whose expense? Because all humor is at somebody's expense. When it's at its best, everyone shoulders a piece of the burden. When it's at its worst, it takes aim at a small, defenseless target. Would it sound like this? "Good evening everybody and welcome to the show. Hey, I just flew in from Hades and boy are my wings tired. (Rimshot) So, anybody here from out of town? (Rimshot) What about these angels, huh? I won't say the angels are a little light in the loafers but when Gabriel starts to blow, whew, they sure take off in a hurry. (Rimshot) No, seriously, I kid the angels but they're a swell bunch of guys, or whatever they are, and so well dressed! (Pause) And that Satan is nuts. Not too bright either. Prince of Darkness, gosh I'm so impressed. He's got his own realm and he doesn't even make himself King. (Rimshot) Now our host on the other hand, this is quite a guy. Let's have a nice round of applause for, God! (Polite, scattered applause) I'll let you in on a little secret. God is actually a very shy guy. And the way things have been going on earth, he's also getting very insecure. How would you feel if people said they liked you but they cheated on you behind your back every chance they got? So if you happen to see him as you're strolling 'round heaven one day, tell him something encouraging, like, 'Gosh, you're much younger than I would've thought,' or, 'nice suit.' It'll help him with his self image. After all, a God with a self-esteem problem brings everybody down. Speaking of a bring down, you should have seen the look on blues legend Little Walter's face when they handed him his harp! (Rimshot) He tried and tried but there was no way he could fit that thing into his mouth." Comedy in heaven, it's a concept, it could work, after all they probably need something to help them pass the time, since it's eternal. But folks.

I'll do the trappings for Paula because she's seven and Christmastime is magic for children. That's different. She believes in a Sanity Claus. Marx your calendars. From now on all my contracts will contain a sanity clause. Yes, I'm bitter. Yes, I'm hurt. Yes, I'm angry. Yes, I want to hurt the world back for being such a shithole. Christmas is a mean joke when you're dispossessed. They're singing songs of joy and peace but there's no peace for me. I can't even sit still. My thoughts race like trash blown down cold, deserted streets. Christmas is not a sweet time when you have nobody and you don't know who you are.

If the world ignores its savior, the one it professes to love, the birthday boy, what the hell is it going to do to a speck on the wall like me? The windows of Wannamaker's are dazzling displays of red and green, tinsel, lights and wrapping paper. But in an alley nearby the urchins pass a bottle and huddle for warmth behind a dumpster.

I left the comfort of my house to read the night sky for a sign but there was nothing.

A cold, blank moon stared back at me. A cloud passed by and partially obscured it. It was really cold outside, cold enough to kill. The stars are just cheap glitter tossed carelessly across a pool of ink. There's no meaning there, no answer. No celestial street sign I can use to navigate my camel to the sacred place, the place of redemption.

Odd to think now of John Lennon and Yoko Ono singing, We wish you good Christmas, and a Happy New Year, we hope it's a good one, without any fear. Without any fear.

Chapter 16

Won't Somebody Please Notice That I'm Sick?

I've been in the advertising business for sixteen years. It's a fun way to make a living. You meet a lot of really intelligent, really original, and really bizarre people. That's the best part. You also get paid for being creative, that's what got me into it in the first place. I've written ads for racehorses, antique clocks, tax shelters, vintage automobiles, hot air balloon weekends, even bulletproof vests. I've worked for DuPont, TV Guide, Prudential, CertainTeed, various small ad agencies, and of course, Honeywell. I've written and produced about every kind of advertising there is, from lavish videos to business cards. I've seen a lot of advertising.

The Manic behavior of that fearsome winter was a form of advertising unique in my experience. It was as though my subconscious mind was doing everything in its power to get help for itself. To get help for me. All my actions seemed tailor-made to draw attention, to lead people to the conclusion that I was mad. My insanity was *not* invisible, I didn't lock myself up safely in a tower, out of harm's way. I flaunted my madness, almost daring anyone to point out the obvious. Was my subconscious mind that smart? I think it was. I think it got help for me at last. But first it needed to get my attention. That required a fist, a boot, and a very mean man.

When I was Manic I was the world's *worst* listener. The defensive wall of bizarre behavior I built around myself, the battlements, did not allow words in. They only allowed a constant torrent of words out. I knew everything. I was endlessly entertaining. The important question was the extent to which everyone was being delighted by me and acknowledging it. The idea that another person had a piece of useful advice that I might want to listen to was ludicrous. I didn't need advice. I gave advice.

But if I knew so much and was so sure of myself, why was my behavior so desperate? So needy? It was just the false confidence of Mania. True confidence, so they say, is so quiet that it's practically silent. I had no confidence at all, about anything. My daughter, my home, my livelihood, my safety, my health, my income, my future. Nothing. I was flailing like a drowning man who grabs onto anything around him. Flailing wildly because inside my soul, inside my heart, was a temple of pure terror. The terror of the man who has walked to the edge of the cliff and gazed down into the burning eternity of Hell. Then turns around only to stare into Satan's eyes. Panic. Terror.

Hopelessness.

I'm just an amateur. Just because I see a shrink doesn't mean that I am a shrink. But this is how I see it. My subconscious mind, accustomed to working in murky, indirect ways, took time to notice the change in me. After all, it left the day-to-day care and feeding of Alistair McHarg to the conscious mind which had a very good track record of being reliable. But this sudden change of style was impossible to deny. All the self-preservation techniques seemed to be gone. In their place, only self-destructive behavior.

At last, the subconscious mind said, "That's it! I've had enough of this bullshit to last me a lifetime! I've got to get this crazy motherfucker out from behind the wheel fast or he's gonna' get *all of us* killed." But every action had to be passed through the filter of the demented, conscious mind.

So, to the conscious mind, Invisible Driving was a brilliant and fun piece of performance art. To the subconscious mind, Invisible Driving was a way of flying a giant distress flag, sending an SOS across the airwaves, shooting up flares at night. It hoped to draw the attention of someone who would put an end to the madness. A sympathetic soul, who understood the pain of mental illness. A knowledgeable soul, who knew the difference between out-of-control and evil. A kind soul, who understood that I was merely a victim of my own genetic design.

The wild humor, the endless laughter, took the place of crying. All the acting out was a kind of crying. The kind of crying which evokes sympathy. The kind of crying which evokes a hug. Except that when expressed this way it evoked no sympathy at all.

My emotions were so volatile that at one moment I could be ecstatically supercharged happy, then, a poignant song on the radio would plunge me instantly into fits of sobbing. There was an aching core of hurt in me, of sorrow and of pain. It was causing me to go to the outer edge of sanity. I needed somebody to see that I needed help, but I didn't know how to ask. I was crying for help, but it didn't look like it.

My malfunctioning mind was telling me I was fine. In fact I was in desperate shape. My subconscious mind at last found a way to get the help I needed.

Chapter 17

I Just Discovered A New Way To Play Chinese Checkers

As I was getting dressed to go see Claire, the phone rang. It occurred to me that it was amazing that the phone was still in service, considering how long it had been since I'd paid the bill. It was Zelda. It might just as well have been the Mayor of Bat Attack, North Dakota for all it meant to me. Incredible how quickly things were fading into the past. She called, she said, to wish me a happy new year. Why hadn't I called? When was the freelance job going to be done, her client was in a hurry. All I could think of was how to get her off the phone with the minimum amount of awkwardness. She called me a bastard for leaving her high and wet. That night at the Barclay I had felt very close to her, now she was just a piece of the past intruding on the present. She wanted to know when we could get together again, she wanted to talk. She wants to talk, I thought, that's rich. When you're hot, everybody wants a piece of you. Later for you, Zelda. You're in the stable now, you're one of the thoroughbreds. Now you work for me. I'll turn you out perhaps, but you don't get me anymore. Other guys would kill to have you, you're throwing yourself at me, I'm looking for my hat. Life sure is funny, isn't it? Just when you think you have it figured out, you don't. I let her babble as my thoughts roamed on like this, finally managing to extricate myself from her verbal talons. Zelda. It was great fun, but it was just one, of those things. Like Eric Dolphy said about the music, you play it, then it's gone.

Out the door. Posmondillip. Snow was beginning to fall as I got into the car for the drive to Claire's. I love the sight of falling snow, I prefer it immensely to the sight of rising snow which I find rather disturbing. But folks, I'm working here, is this thing on? It transforms how everything looks. The world becomes different, the same, yet different. That was the deal with me. The world was the same, but I was different, so it seemed different too. I crept along the roads cautiously, an all black car moving stealthily in an all white world. By the time I was at Claire's I was in an all white car in an all black world.

I've always had trouble taking New Year's seriously as a holiday, perhaps because of my WASP background. How can you get enthused about a holiday where people honor an arbitrary moment on a clock by dressing formally, drinking to the point of stupidity, kissing strangers, and finishing off with a flourish of fatal automobile accidents? My idea of celebrating the New Year is surviving the old one.

Claire's street looked considerably less threatening dressed in white. I parked my car and walked slowly to the house, marveling at the wonderful way snow has of absorbing sound. It didn't just look white, it sounded white. I was entering another world. All around me was quiet and pure. I would have to make myself pure too. Drain off the bile. Shed the dreck that had accumulated and covered my flesh. The expectations. The prejudices. The bourgeois banality that had grown on me like a fungus. I rang Claire's doorbell with a bag full of champagne under my arm, a pocketful of joints, and a sense that I was about to leave the country for a long time.

She let me in and we shared a long kiss, it was a giddy, bubbly moment. I brushed off my camel coat and hung it in the vestibule, wonderful, these old houses. A vestibule, with a door. In the living room Prince Wilson and Ultraviolet were tuning large, African drums. There were instruments everywhere, not the kind you buy in music stores. They had a rough, hand hewn look. Very beautiful. Normally in a social situation like this I would shake hands, make polite conversation, and the like. But with these people, I didn't know how to act. I took my cue from Claire, who made no move to introduce me to them. Well, I thought, when in Rome cheer gleefully as you watch an hysterical Christian torn into pieces by a pride of half-starved lions, as the old saying goes. She just led me towards the staircase. When I asked her if I should put the champagne on ice she said she had everything we needed upstairs. That sounded promising so I followed. I felt as though I glowed with energy. When she opened the door to her suite of rooms on the third floor, I was totally amazed. If a pregnant opossum had tried to come in after us, she would have given birth on the spot, her babies would have been squeezed right out of her. The hallway was so crammed full of shit it was almost impossible to walk through it. This is what it would look like, I thought, if a twelve-year-old child lived in an adult's house and never cleaned up after herself. Boxes were stacked on bureaus reaching all the way to the ceiling. There were dirty plates and glasses everywhere. A maze of phone wires and extension cords curled down the hall like tangled plastic snakes. She showed me the front room, a huge space with tall windows. It was possible to see the floor in only one point, obviously where she stood to paint.

There were canvases everywhere, coffee cans filled with brushes, plastic milk crates used as shelves, complete chaos. And dirt. Everything was filthy. In one corner of the room stood several department store mannequins, squeezed together. Each was wearing several hats, but nothing else. Bookshelves sagged. The entire place looked like it was put together with chewing gum, baling wire, and rubber bands. Everything was cheap and crummy. Nothing matched. Nothing looked like it had been bought new, as though it had all been left behind by people who were moving out. I was stunned but kept my judgmental observations to myself. She led me down the hall and pointed to her bedroom, the door was open. It looked like a squirrel's nest. A huge mattress lay on the floor. Like the workroom, the entire bedroom was covered with debris, I couldn't see any part of the floor. Books, clothes, records, random papers formed a complete blanket covering the carpet, assuming that there was carpeting. Then she took me to the back. There was a bathroom with a door that could barely open since a tall bureau stood next to it. And there was a sitting room. This is where she had her TV. Of the entire floor, this was the only room which offered a place to sit, except for the bathroom, or so I hoped. There was a couch of sorts, a wafer thin mattress which rested on some cinderblocks, and an easy chair covered in a fabric of such profound vulgarity that the designer must surely have hung himself out of shame. This was obviously the room she had designated for us as I saw glasses and a waste paper basket filled with ice. I put the champagne bottles in it and sat down. The waste paper basket was forest green and had an oval shaped depiction of a fox hunt on its side. A dashing man in a red riding jacket and black hat was whipping his horse as it jumped over a stone wall. For the first time since laying eyes on Claire's quarters, I laughed.

Claire looked at me with modesty, almost apologetically. "I don't normally let people up here," she said. "You have to understand, my work is everything. I just don't have time for cleaning." She sat down on the rocking chair, happily hiding most of the fabric from my view. I offered her a joint. She took it and lit it. Aha, I thought, she likes to smoke pot. This chick is perfect, she likes all the same things I do. And look at this house! If nothing else, the condition of this house declares loud and clear, here you may do whatever you want. I've always loved to travel and there, on the third floor of Claire's house, I felt as though I was in not just another country but another reality. A reality where creativity is king and bourgeois morality is banished. I had the most peculiar sensation of homecoming.

We passed the joint back and forth, she seemed calm, as though she already knew me well. I asked her how she'd done at the Bourse, if she'd sold anything.

"Lousy," she said without rancor, "I barely made back the fee." She paused and then said matter of factly, "My stuff never sells well, nobody gets it."

"That's incredible," I said, "it's so wonderful, it's so funny." This was not flattery in the service of seduction, this was sincere. It was Claire's work that had grabbed me.

"Well, thanks," she said in a tone that attempted to fend off the compliment. "I do it for me, it's my healing. If other people like it, that's just gravy."

I studied the response. Claire sounded wise to me, as though she was light years ahead of me. "Let's not wait 'til twelve for the champagne," I said, "let's have some now." I opened a bottle, making sure to remove the cork not with a pop like some idiotic ball player after winning the World Series, (a phrase which has always amazed me since the World isn't involved, just another example of the mind-boggling self importance of the United States), but with a satisfying sigh, not spilling a drop. I noticed that the glasses didn't match. Jesus Christ, I thought, this chick must do all her shopping at yard sales. Is this poverty or is it a political statement? I held up my glass and clinked it against hers.

"To us," I said, thinking it the most appropriate toast possible.

"Surrender, madness, and creation," was her toast. It didn't make me feel more secure in the relationship but it did set me thinking. We let the champagne tickle us. There's a word for you, tickle. A world without tickling wouldn't be worth having. I was beginning to feel more comfortable. I was ecstatic, but not frantic. Entranced perhaps. I studied Claire for the first time, just in case there was going to be an exam later. But folks. There was a serenity to her, she spoke rarely, I did all the talking. She was not a great beauty, not in the same class as the litter of kittens I'd been playing with in recent days. Straight hair, parted in the middle, swooping down just beyond her shoulders. Big, dark eyes, perhaps her best feature. An aquiline, aristocratic nose and thin lips. Nice cheekbones, although not particularly pronounced. Medium height, small breasted, fairly wide hips and somewhat chunky thighs. In pieces she was unspectacular, taken together there was something strangely powerful about her presence, a squatchiness, an aura perhaps, composure. She wore absolutely no makeup at all, earrings seemed to be her only concession to feminine trappings. Amazingly, she was dressed as before, sweater, turtleneck and jeans. She was presentable but it was almost as though she was trying to hide her femininity. And she certainly hadn't gone out of her way to dress seductively in any traditional sense. Still, she held a powerful attraction for me, I wanted her as much as ever.

I asked her if I could take off my shoes and she said sure. Surveying the random clutter of the room I found a tiny place on the floor that I staked out as mine. Surrounded by chaos and license as I was, I was prissy, fussy, and meticulous. I placed the shoes neatly together, side-by-side, pointing in the same direction. Everything had to be just so. I had staked a claim. Unable to sit still, excited by the prospect of being with her, I couldn't help but fuss. Mr. Fidget. I emptied my pockets, a favorite pastime, and neatly placed the contents in my shoes. I could have been in the Marines judging by the devotion to order I was expressing. Not satisfied, I removed my watch and put it in my shoes as well. She observed without a comment. Was I removing the artifacts of the world I was leaving behind, so that I could surrender myself totally to hers? There wasn't much left between us, only clothes.

I babbled on and on, weaving dizzily from one theme to the next. The need to free James Brown. My happiness at leaving the corporate world and my desire to become a performance artist. My theory that to begin the road to greatness one first had to hit absolute zero. My feelings about music, how I might become the first great WASP blues singer. My chatter was a crazy quilt held together only by energy, but she seemed to find it fascinating. The last few hours of the year were draining away, there was no rush to make love, only talk, seduction by voice, strange powers of speech, touch seduces the flesh but talk seduces the mind. We were reaching into each other, becoming one. The champagne continued to flow, she lit candles and incense. Lit incense for Christ's sake, I felt as though I'd shed twenty years and awoken in college during the days of Flower Power. Still, it had the desired effect, forgotten for so long, of creating a surreal, woozy sensuality. As long as we're crossing the line, may as well get the nose into the act too. (I'd also like the nose to make an appearance in Act III). I was beginning to sweat. I took off my sweater and carefully folded it up. By the time I was done it looked like it had just come out of the box. I placed it carefully, precisely next to the shoes. Having established a beachhead, I now claimed enough floorspace as mine to also accommodate a sweater.

"I'm so happy," I said, "I want to cry. I'd given up hope of ever finding somebody who could understand me."

Claire smiled. "Maybe the timing was just right," she said softly. "I've been alone for a long while too, buried in my work." If birds had appeared from the ceiling and started tying ribbons in her hair I don't think it would have surprised me at all. Things that never happen were happening. I was falling in love, it seemed completely improbable but perhaps that was the proof that it was real. We kissed at last, for the first time since she had greeted me at the door. If the two of us had risen up in the air, like Rilke's perfect lovers, I think I would have merely observed that apparently, in Claire's house, the law of gravity had been repealed. In Claire's house, magic was real.

"Claire," I said, "I'm yours. *If* you want to make love, *when* you want to make love, *how* you want to make love, are all up to you. Just tell me." I was so far out on a limb, anything could've happened. The pot, the champagne, the romance, the feeling of foreignness were all swirling together and making me nozzmondilik. Whereas with the other women I'd felt a compulsion to control, with Claire, I felt a need to surrender. To let go.

She studied me, then came close and said, "Stay here, I'll be right back." With that she used the door connecting the sitting room with her bedroom, leaving me alone to wonder what she had in store. I took the opportunity to use the bathroom, squeezing through the door, pushing it against the bureau as far as it would go. This entire place is a study in constipation, I thought, it's congested with crap and she can't let any of it go. I hungered for white space. I imagined a white room with only one chair in it. The bathroom was no better. Paint was peeling off the walls and the ceiling. It was filthy. There were cans of cleaning products but they looked like they'd never been touched. Even they had dirt on them. As I was washing my hands, as tidy as a raccoon, I stared at myself in the mirror. "Alistair," I said to myself, looking into my own red eyes, "you are just too funny. How the hell did you ever find this place?" I laughed with a curious combination of giddy anticipation and genuine bemused disbelief. Apparently there were still plenty of new, interesting experiences left in store for me. I went back into the sitting room and lit another joint. I began to pace. I stared out the window. Snow was still falling, masking the squalor below. Then Claire reentered the room from her bedroom, closing the door behind her.

She stood in front of the door and stopped. I feasted my hungry eyes on her. She was wearing a full-length white gown made out of some sort of transparent gauze, even in the candlelight I could see that she was naked underneath. The gown was covered with all sorts of symbols, sewn on, made of silver cloth. There were crescent moons, meteors, pentagrams, faces, she looked like some sort of sensuous sorceress.

"My God," I said, "you're gorgeous." I focused in on her pert, sweet breasts, plainly visible. Her hard nipples pointed through the thin film of the fabric.

She looked at me for several moments before saying, "*You're* gorgeous." She took my hand and stood me in front of a full-length mirror that I'd noticed before. It had seemed odd to me at the time a woman clearly lacking in vanity would have such a large mirror in her room. She stood behind so I could see her too. If she tells me to walk through that goddamned mirror like some kind of Cocteau movie, I thought, I quit.

"Alistair," she said in that low, sexy voice of hers, "listen to me." I liked to hear her use my name. "It all begins with loving yourself." I looked at her eyes in the mirror, not understanding what she wanted or what she was getting at. She was putting me through something I didn't understand, teaching me something. Now I was being controlled. Was this some sort of bizarre ceremony? The randiness of the moment was provoking a nightstick so hard that a cop could have used it to break up a bar fight.

School's out, I can do anything I want. My heart was banging in my chest like a bird trying to beat its way out of a glass cage. Lightheaded, flippy, gone, rabazibby. Floating, floating, floating high above the real world. Napazoopie. Maybe there isn't just one reality, maybe there are thousands coexisting. Maybe you can flip from one into another like changing channels on a television set. Who knows? I certainly felt like I'd slipped through a trap door and dropped into another dimension. I had no idea if it was 1990 yet, it could have been 9109 for all I cared about time. I was completely immersed in the present.

"I'm hungry," I said, "I need something to eat." Only at that moment did I realize that we hadn't eaten anything all evening. Christ, I thought, maybe she doesn't cook either. Of course, since I never ate, this wouldn't present much of a problem. Or maybe, like me, she was just more interested in us than in food.

"What would you like?" she asked, in a dreamy, faraway voice. I kissed her.

"Something delicious," I replied, kissing her nipples through the fabric. I planted a delicate kiss on her stomach and eased her onto the floor, squirming down next to her. I shed my remaining clothes like a rattlesnake slithering out of his scales. "Something pink." I lifted the gown, watching the candlelight shimmer off the silver fabric of the decorations. With tiny kisses as gentle as spring rain I started heading down. I lay on the floor, face buried, and began.

I had all the time in the world. I was in no hurry to make her come, there were no goals for the evening. She rubbed my head as I luxuriated. Slorch. Slorch. Slorch. If it had taken an hour it would have been fine with me. Maybe it did. She began to whine in time to the tongue-lashing and then. Imagine a steam locomotive at full throttle running into a brick wall. Okay, now imagine a squid in a sandwich bag reciting Dylan Thomas poems, it's not relevant, but it's kind of fun.

"Whoa, whoa, whoa, aaaaaaaa," she wailed, lost in it, gone in it, "whoa, whoa, aaaaaaa," body all focused on that one pleasure point, "whoa, whoa, aaaaaaa," so good, so good, better than anything ever could be, "whoa."

She slumped back. I moved up and put my snozzle inside her, it was thick as a bookie's bankroll. After a woman has had her first orgasm, the second comes easily, so to speak, the third more easily still. It's the first one that's tough. Smooth and slippy, smooth and slippy, good and plenty, good and plenty, baby let me be your chauffeur, I wanna be your chauffeur, drive you all, drive you all over town. I was driving Claire around the world. Our first time. It had to be magic. It had to be unforgettable, it had to be just exactly what we wanted it to be. Uhhh. I wanted us to both go off at once. To both go off the edge of the earth at once. To go off to the moon at once. Good mornin' little schoolgirl. Uhhh. Good mornin' little schoolgirl. Uhhh. Can I go home? Baby, can I go home with you? Uhhh. I'll tell your mama and your papa, I'm a little schoolboy too.

I opened my eyes and looked at Claire's face. Her forehead was furrowed in intense concentration. She let go her second orgasm, not quite as powerful as the first, but deeper. She was grinding against me, squirming around so that I squizzled inside her. I let go. Timing is everything. Add timing to the list of things that are everything along with details, music, honesty and finding a good parking spot. I felt so good coming inside Claire that I didn't know what to do first, set my hair on fire or learn to speak Chinese. I'd found my kitten to end all kittens. My new home. It was weird, but I could do anything. Even turn this shithole into a palace, the kind of place befitting the kitten who had been designated to assume the place next to me on the throne. We both nodded off after the earthquake orgasm. I woke up first, of course. We tottered off together into the squirrel's nest that was Claire's bedroom. I marveled at the place. Doing an inventory of a hardware store would have taken less time than doing an inventory of Claire's bedroom. We nestled like spoons in her bed. Let it snow, I thought, I hope it's a foot deep by morning. I was engulfed in Claire's room like a womb. I put my arms around her and snuggled, the two of us, entwined, naked, back to front, hurtling through space together into the uncertainty of a new year, a new decade, a new posnogomy.

Chapter 18

The Seductive Call Of All That Is Not Me

One of the highlights of my career as a jazz listener was a concert in Carnegie Hall. It featured McCoy Tyner and his big band, the outrageous Pharaoh Sanders, and the immortal one himself, Rahsaan Roland Kirk. The hall was hushed as McCoy Tyner, pianist for John Coltrane during the legendary quartet years, took the stage with his large and heavily armed band. Nothing sounds prettier than a room holding hundreds of people with their mouths shut. It reminded me of the Quaker meetings I used to go to every week at school. So many people, alone with their thoughts, together in a room, silent. Great moment. The wooden floors of the old hall creaked like a ship at sea as people settled in their seats. This silence was not the silence of a bus station at 3:00 AM in the morning. This was warm and rich, the audience filled with respect, even awe, and anticipation. You could have heard a lemon drop drop.

And then, we heard a bomb drop. Tyner's band burst into an all-stops-out barrage of sound intensity that blew off every hairpiece in the room. From silence to a hurricane of sound, cracking and crashing like madness, so loud that it couldn't be denied, it didn't come in through your ears, it came in through your bones. I felt like I was having an orgasm. I was so relieved, so joyful, so happy, I wanted to jump to my feet, thrust my fists into the air and scream "Yes! Thank you!"

Later, when I was replaying the concert in my mind, I wondered about that moment. Why was it that I craved that level of intensity so much? The longer I thought about it, the harder it became to avoid my best theory. The music was so strong, it obliterated my personality. It was so complete, so overwhelming, that it freed me from myself. I was immersed in only the intoxication of the music. I forgot about me.

In one way or the other, I've been doing that all my life. Running from my personality instead of making the best of it. In the intoxication of romance, I lost myself. Escape into depression, another kind of flight. Escape into isolation, cutting myself off from other people. (And then actually having the nerve to feel sorry for myself because I was alone!) Escape into drugs, alcohol, sex, reading, art. More important, escape into failure. Failure was the ultimate comfort, the ultimate safety. If I was a loser I wouldn't have to worry about other people because nobody would pay any attention to me.

Because of my natural gifts, assets, and training, true failure evaded me at first and I occasionally tripped onto success by mistake. But, through a subconscious determination to fail, to kick away life's pleasures at all cost, I achieved it at last.

Such extreme perversity needs explanation. Mine has a name. Ian Lennox McHarg. My father's genius, vision, craving for acceptance, and maniacal energy helped him forge a dazzling career. This is what he did for a living. He was a professor of Landscape Architecture and Regional Planning at the University of Pennsylvania. He was also the Chairman of that department for thirty years. He was an author. (His first book, Design With Nature, is a bible in its field and is being translated into Chinese even as I write this.) He was a partner in a world-renowned architectural firm called Wallace, McHarg, Roberts & Todd. (A firm which began on the third floor of the house I grew up in.) He was a non-stop lecturer, pounding the lectern in defense of the environment year after year. He hosted a TV interview show called "The House We Live In," where he interviewed celebrated intellectuals like Paul Tillich. On those rare occasions when he was home, he spent time not with us, but in the garden, planting trees, moving stones, filling ponds, and building brick paths.

Unfortunately, the crest of his career coincided with my departure for college. Just when I should have been separating from my family, building my own identity, was precisely when he was impossible to avoid. LIFE Magazine came to our house and did a story, complete with photos. He turned up on the radio, on TV, and in print with relentless regularity. Whenever I was introduced at a party, the automatic response was, "Oh, are you any relation to Ian McHarg?" At first it seemed like a cheap way to get attention, unearned attention. Then it became like a curse, following me wherever I went. I came to understand that the price was very high indeed. The price was nothing less than my self.

I quickly concluded that I could never compete with him. He was just too big. My personality, with all of its insecurities, just didn't have the firepower to remove him from his throne, the way every son must. So, without even realizing it, I gave up on the idea of pushing myself as hard as I could and going as far as I could. I settled for surviving, I didn't go for home runs. (Of course I wasn't above trading on my father's fame when it suited me, I was that sleazy and insecure. I'd casually refer to Lewis Mumford, Howard Nemerov, Averill Harriman, Charles Addams, and Louis Kahn as though they were friends of *mine*, not my father's. Even today I occasionally trot out the photograph of me shaking hands with President Bush and offhandedly recall the time I had lunch at the White House with him, B.B. King, Jasper Johns, Beverly Sills, and just a handful of others.) My personality was becoming more and more bent. I could tell you a thousand things that were wrong with me, but a pat on my back would've burst my lungs.

I was trapped in an unholy dynamic. First, I believed that I had to be as great as him for it to count. Nothing less than stellar success would be good enough. Next, I was certain that I didn't have the raw materials to soar that high. The intelligence, perhaps. The creativity, perhaps. The soul, perhaps. But the one thing I was certain that I didn't have was the balls. Everything about him said MAN. Decorated war hero. Youngest Major in the British Army. Paratrooper. Spent most of his time behind enemy lines. He looked bullet-proof, fearless. Compared to him I was a pampered powder-puff, raised in luxury in post-war America, a stranger to struggle.

I was the judge and the jury. I found myself lacking, I was guilty of being a wimp. I sentenced myself to a life of mediocrity. My self-esteem drooped and shriveled like a sapling deprived of light by an enormous shadow.

That was the personality I ended up with. That was the personality I needed so desperately to escape.

Chapter 19

Street Level

Much of the cavernous emptiness of my days is spent walking. Giant strides. Giant steps. That's one for you John Coltrane, you're the boss. The activity of walking fills time, which is good, because time is an empty vessel sailing nowhere, burns energy, and provides me with Khan, Chaka Khan, pro and con, stant stimulation. I'm almost always downtown, roaming the streets day and night. With my intensity, speed, and determination I must look like I'm on my way to an important appointment but in fact I'm just walking, experiencing, squizzling, being. Part of the play, part of the action, the dark of the day, the dissatisfaction. If I see a beautiful woman I walk a few paces behind her and sing something soulful for her benefit, it's a free benefit concert. Get it? A Stevie Wonder selection for example. If it's magic, then why can't it be everlasting? Something tender. Singing not to be heard but to be overheard. I love to watch them prick up their ears. Always ready to inject the unexpected element of zapbopadoopie into the equation. No pickup attempted, just a little musical kiss blown into the breeze. Spinning a gossamer web of seduction. When you love music the way I do, love it good, love it real good, love it toe-suckin' good, it shows. People respond. I receive smiles, coy body language, the quivering slishing of kittens which absolutely sends me off, bemused appreciation, a thousand little strokes of approval. Exquisite torture. Give that man a thousand lashes, a thousand eye lashes. Rip off his shirt and give him a thousand strokes, a thousand strokes of approval. Always performing, always giving. No money changes hands but there's currency all the same. Yes, I acknowledge that you exist, yes, you're a surprise, yes, that's a beautiful song.

Walking the streets of downtown Philadelphia I encounter bums, lunatics, hookers, drug addicts and homeless wretches on a regular basis. Since I'm almost always smoking I'm very put out, don't fire, I get hit on for cigarettes constantly. My money is dwindling to a point where a pack of cigarettes is a major purchase so I can't afford to be as generous as I'd like but still I give many away. But I won't do it without turning it into a mini-set. I stop my runaway pace, something akin to halting a cheetah in hot pursuit, and I know a cheetah when I see one, compose myself. I search my pockets for cigarettes, no mean feat in itself. After finding them I hold one out and just as I'm handing it over I assume a very solemn look, which may be a mistake because it's dangerous to assume anything, and say something along the lines of, "I feel that I should warn you that these things are very bad for your health." Oh God how I amuse myself. Even if no one else thinks it's funny, I sure do. Giving a warning like this to a person who's shooting dope or eating out of garbage pails by comparison. I usually supply them with a book of Four Seasons matches as well, details are everything. Or else, "Did you ever try quitting?" As if to say, if you can't afford them maybe you should consider not needing them. Frequently this provokes a laugh and a laugh can be very dangerous when it's provoked. If I can make a homeless person laugh, make them happy for even an instant, I've done something remarkable. I'm taking my act on the road, right down onto the street, and it keeps working. I can work any room in the city, from the Bellevue to the subway stations of the cross and irritable. I'm that good. Incredibly good. So good I have to slap my own face so I don't get too cocky. Waifs are not used to being treated like people, individuals, they're used to being treated like things. They see me in my camel coat and figure me for just another three-piece button down Brooks Brothers bonehead. How little they know.

All over the city I see bums sleeping, despite the bitter cold, heads on the pavement, covered with heaps of foul blankets. One of my best mini-sets depends on walking past one of them just as some super square slatch-head businessman is coming towards me. Just at the point when we're both looking at the bum contemptuously I yell, in a fierce, imperious tone of voice, "That's it Fred, if I catch you sleeping on the job one more time, you're fired!" The look of horror on the businessman's face makes it all worthwhile.

I had another mini-set recently I really liked. There's an intersection I pass frequently because it's close to the Four Seasons which is home to three street people and in an odd way I too am one. Very territorial these types. Stake out a claim with milk carton boxes, blankets, cardboard. There's a steam vent there. I was coming down the sidewalk towards them one brutally cold, sunny morning just a few days ago. It's a bus-stop and there was quite a crowd of downtown businessmen and women. Attaché cases. Shoes so shiny you could shave in the reflection. Gorgeous wool coats, scarves, if good grooming is a virtue then these people were in the passing lane headed for heaven. What a disturbing contrast. At their feet were these three forlorn souls, broken and bent, clinging onto life alone. No question about quality of life. If they lived, they'd beaten the system and the way they lived was giving their systems a beating. Like trained monkeys they held out their begging cups, discarded coffee cups from a nearby 7-11. The words came out on their own, it was totally unplanned. I don't have to try anymore, it's automatic, I'm walking art.

I looked into the first one's cup and said loudly enough for the entire group to hear, "Let's see, you've only got a quarter."

Then I looked into the next one's cup. "My Gosh, you don't have anything at all."

The third cup. "Let's see, three pennies, a nickel, and two quarters. That's fifty-eight cents."

I paused for a moment and then addressed all three of them, since for the time being they had no address. "You know, you guys aren't doing very well. Perhaps you should consider getting a little more ambitious, and going into *crime*, like these people." With that I swept my arm around grandly indicating the crowd, which by now was looking at me, and them, with appalled expressions. Fuck 'em. Let 'em be horrified. Homelessness exists, you can't make it go away by ignoring it. The man said, whatever you do don't grin, you'll give the game away. Procol Harum, a Latin phrase. Why am I the only one who knows all these things? I've taken that on as my special assignment. Blowing the whistle. Giving the game away. Why isn't truth a four-letter word?

My exchanges with beggars are personal, direct. Where most people toss a coin into a cup and move along quickly, careful to avoid eye contact, I honor these people by treating them like people. Sometimes that means being hard on them but at least I don't treat them like beasts, like aliens. If a bum, sitting on the sidewalk, asks for money I'm equally capable of either giving him some or snapping back, "Fuck you, get a job." This startles many of them accustomed as they are to either being ignored or satisfied with some token, either bus or subway.

One young guy looked genuinely hurt and asked, "Why do you say that?"

Without an instant of hesitation I said, "Because you're whole, for Chrissake. Look at you. You're young, you're not missing any arms or legs, you're still healthy. You're just a fuckin' bum. There are people out here on the street who couldn't be anywhere else. They're crippled. They're blind, they're insane. You're stealing money from them. Get a job you sack a shit, you're cluttering up my sidewalk." The poor fellow was stunned. As I turned away from him I saw the most beatific, that's right, beatific, look on the face of a Korean man who, unknown to me, had watched the exchange. He held out his hand and shook mine enthusiastically.

Smiling he said, "I agree with you." At some point you have to stop blaming other people for the quagmire you're in whether you're black or white, rich or poor. When that moment arrives you can finally kiss childhood goodbye.

Late one night I was working my way through town, burning up shoe leather, and I saw the doorman at the Barclay talking to another man. Doormen, I thought, must surely be as worldly wise as bartenders. Doormen see it all. I decided to try my hypothesis.

Slowing down my pace I interrupted them with, "Excuse me fellows but do you know where I could get a good blowjob for under fifty dollars?"

They both looked at me, then looked at each other, and then the doorman, without missing a beat said, "Sure, just go down to city hall, the city council specializes in that sort of thing." Bless you, I thought, you're so good. I laughed out loud, the three of us shared a laugh in the darkness of Rittenhouse Square. The shorthand had said so much. Get on the bus immediately. Some people are with it. I don't care about the quantity of my audience but I want the quality to be as good as it gets. Naparoopy.

Chapter 20

You Can't Catch Me, I'm The Gingerbread Man

One of my most visceral memories of that Manic episode was the feeling of movement. Intense, rapid, constant movement. Endless, round-the-clock, pointless. Walking, talking, driving, entering and leaving. As long as I was moving, I didn't have to face my illness. As long as I was racing into one piece of busywork after another, I didn't have to confront the fear that had provoked the episode. As long as I was racing away, sustaining the chimera of happiness, the sadness didn't have a chance to settle. I was outrunning reality.

All three of my major episodes have had this element of terrified flight. In each case, a catastrophic event triggered a reaction, my mind began to run. Instead of facing the problem, my mind played the Manic sleight of hand, "now you see it, now you don't." By creating the false euphoria, the problem disappeared. I was the ostrich, head in sand, behind dangerously exposed. Or the small child being teased by bullies. He sticks his thumbs in his ears, closes his eyes, and chants in a whiny, nasal voice, "Nyah nyah nyah nyah nyah nyah, I caaaaan't hear you." It works for a while, until the bullies get mad and beat the Fig Newtons out of him. Flight just doesn't work. My father, in a rare moment of insight considering he believes all psychiatrists are quacks, once said to me, "No matter where you go, you take your problems with you." Fearsome words, true words, relevant to me. Because I had spent a lifetime running.

When I was Manic I ran like a cheetah. When I was sound, mildly depressed, I ran in slow motion, like a Sumo wrestler chasing an ice cream truck. But running is running, regardless of the speed. And I was not running *towards* anything, I was running *away*.

That my father holds psychiatrists in contempt angers the hell out of me because psychiatrists played an essential role in me saving my own life. Without psychiatrists and psychotropic medicine I cannot guarantee that I would be alive today. I'm a great fan of psychiatry. But one of the most hurtful criticisms I ever heard was from a psychiatrist, he said I was the victim of a "Peter Pan syndrome." That one really cut me down to nothing. The implication, of course, was that I refused to grow up. What I was running from, was adulthood. I despised him for making this observation because I knew he was right. I was like everyone else in the respect that I admired the truth until it came to the truth about my own shortcomings.

The running became clear. I was running from adulthood, from the responsibilities of adulthood. Running from taking command of my own life. I was running from the showdown with my father, the showdown where I said, "Move over, old timer, sit down. Your day is past. There's a new Sheriff in town and I'm him. Now relax and let me show you and the rest of the world what I can do." Running from my own, deficient personality, running from looking at it honestly, running from forging it into the very best it could be. Running from the work that would take. Running from the fear that went with chancing everything, risking everything, trying as hard as I possibly could. Running from the fear of failure, and worse, the fear of success. So much chickenheartedness breeds so much running.

Running from fate, from destiny. I was not designed and built for failure. The bloodline is good, even with these damnable genes. There's incredible accomplishment on both sides of my lineage. My experience too, is exceptional. (Small thanks to me.) I come by it honestly, I have a great deal to offer. To stop running meant to assume, at last, an appropriate relationship with my surroundings. But for this to happen, I had to learn how to stop running. Manic Depression provided a path.

In Manic Depression I found a problem too big to run away from, it was either face it or let it kill me. In order to face it, I had to mobilize every shred of fiber, every scrap of manliness, I had. This showed me something which amazed me. Far from being a wimp, I had the heart of a lion! Not only was there no question about me being a man, I was a man with an exceptional level of bravery and resolve. Having faced down this vicious killer and won, I hungered for bigger challenges. I became acquainted with my power for the first time, and learned to celebrate it. In a really screwy way, I owe this illness my life. It forced me to grow into my own shoes. It forced me to learn how to give everything.

Chapter 21

Seven Differences Between A Baritone Saxophone And A Kumquat

There may actually be more than seven. For one, you don't need a reed to play a kumquat. I thought of others as I drove home, entranced by the dazzling blue sky, the brilliant white snow and the sparkling sunshine. This was a day constructed in heaven in fact I thought I noticed a few angels in hard hats. It was cold but clear, and besides, what was cold when you'd just met your future? When I pulled into the parking space in front of my townhouse, it looked unfamiliar. It was clean, refined, above all, suburban. The city was going to be my home, the city, where the action was. Where the exceptional reptiles lurked. Where the affluent and indigent, glamorous and grotesque rubbed shoulders and breathed the same air. The bourgeois boredom was too tame to hold me much longer. Against my better instincts I went to the gazebo that housed all the mailboxes for the complex.

The mailman was at the back, quietly filling them, methodically stuffing the missives into the slots as I had been methodically stuffing the snozzle into the slits. Nobody is safe. I talk to everybody and say whatever inspired snerchiness pops into my brain. I eyed him and said, ""But how do you steel yourself against the obstacle of a faultless day?"

"I'm sorry," he said, "I didn't see you there. What did you say?"

"Happy New Year," I responded. "By the way I'm a great defender of the U.S. Postal System even though everyone else likes to take cheap shots at you guys," pause for breath, "I think you do a terrific job when you actually look at the volume of stuff you transport every day it's amazing and the percentage of letters and packages lost, despite what your detractors say, is infinitesimally small."

He looked up at me for the first time. A young, mild mannered white guy, some of my targets don't even have a prayer, it's a wonder they don't have headburns the way my quips zing past them, this was almost too easy.

"Well," he searched for a suitable response, certain that one was expected, "thanks."

Now that I had his attention I fired my salvo. "I've always admired your motto," I continued, starting to rattle it off, "Neither rain nor sleet nor gloom of night nor carnivorous vampire bats shall stay these couriers from the swift depletion of their anointed hounds." He looked up. "Well, I took a few liberties with it but you get my drift."

He mumbled in the affirmative.

"But here's my question. Now if it rains you can prepare by wearing a coat and a hat and if it snows you can put on gloves and boots and if it's dark you can carry a flashlight but how do you steel yourself against the obstacle of a beautiful day?"

He looked up at me with unhappiness in his eyes, unable to understand, unable to escape. My favorite, a captive audience. Baritone saxophones are really hard to juggle. "I don't get the question," he said at last.

"Well," I went on, closing in for the kill, injecting him with a shot of zapadoopie in the midst of his otherwise vapid, that's right he said vapid when a lesser man might have said empty because Alistair always goes the extra yardage Alistair is amazing Alistair is not merely better than most Alistair is the best, day whether he liked it or not, "take a day like today for example. Look at it, it's perfect. What's to prevent you or any other postal person, please note the non-sexist terminology, from saying later for this shmutz I'm taking off today it's too beautiful to work, dropping the old letter bag, and heading off for a wander in the sylvan splendor of the park to admire the flora and fauna? How can you protect yourself against succumbing to a temptation like that? I mean, how about if it read neither rain nor sleet nor gloom of night nor weather of such beatific splendor that it would bring tears to the eyes of an ascetic and tempt the virtue of a saint shall stay these couriers et cetera and like that."

"I guess I never thought of good weather as a problem," said the postman at last.

I emptied my mailbox. It was stuffed like a flounder with crabmeat, back to fishing, can't seem to avoid fishing, ominous envelopes mostly with angry messages on the outside and attention-getting colors. I lost my interest in the postman and let him off the hook, oh God not again, much to his relief I imagine. "Free James Brown," I said to him, my new equivalent of saying goodbye. I was walking back towards the front door of my house when one of my neighbors, a curious-natured retired woman, intercepted me. She was walking her all white miniature poodle. Now, I'm sorry, no I'm not, a golden retriever is a dog, a great dane is a dog, but a miniature poodle is a perverse canine caricature. Miniature poodles don't bark, they nag. Only the human mind could take a wolf, breed it until it looked like a bad throw pillow, and teach it to act like Oscar, I'm dying beyond my means, either that wallpaper goes or I do, Wilde. However, the woman was nice enough and had always been sweet to my daughter Paula and her friend Mary when they bopped around the neighborhood. So I endured her. You're never going to see a kumquat in a pawn shop. Where had I been, she wanted to know, she hadn't seen me around much. So I launched into my story about being let go by Honeywell. She was sympathetic.

I ranted. "Yes, that's right. Right at Christmastime, can you believe it? No income. All my benefits cut. No health insurance. No life insurance." Life insurance, the phrase sounded funny as I said it. I felt a little burst of squatchatopolis go off in the back of my head. I went on, "but I'm not interested in life insurance just now. Actually I'm looking for somebody to sell me death insurance."

"What?" she said. Before she was smiling sympathetically, her look turned to uncertainty.

"Yes," I proceeded, warming to the theme, "death insurance. I'm beginning to get the uneasy feeling that I'm going to live forever, it's bothering me. I'm looking for somebody who can guarantee that sooner or later I'm going to get out of this miserable world."

I said it with robust good humor, heartily amused by the observation. I was, in fact, developing a frightening belief that I was unstoppable. I was laughing about the idea of death insurance as I walked into my house and she walked off with her little companion, yellowing the snow, straining at the leash. On a leash/On a walk around the block/You're the envy of the neighborhood. Poor Hilary, what must she think? The realization that anything is possible creates both saints and sinners.

I looked through the envelopes. I threw away the advertising first. That still left quite a few. I could tell who they were from, nearly all bills. Credit card companies. Electric company. A letter from my landlord. A card from Hilary, pretty envelope. I thought, if I open one I have to open them all. After thinking about it for a long as it takes a freshman Congressman to lose what little integrity he has left, as long as it takes go to become gone, I got up and threw them all in the trash. Kumquats don't set off airport metal detectors. A new age required new solutions, and not just seven percent solutions, one hundred percent solutions. Besides, why throw good money after bad? I was going to move in with Claire, it was so obvious. Why worry about this place? And as far as the credit cards went, get serious. What little money I had left I had to hang onto. For living day-to-day. When things started to fall into place, when the money started to pour in, I'd pay 'em. In the meantime the objective is to stay focused, stay together, keep pushing.

I called Claire at work, reviving my euphoria, for a moment there my euphoria had passed out and I'd had to throw water on it and slap it in the face. We made plans to get together the next day because this was my night to have Paula. Secure that my future lay before me like a castle with the drawbridge down and the portcullis raised, yes portcullis, I set into an afternoon of cataloging, organizing, arranging. It wouldn't do to have Paula over when the house was a mess. I picked her up early from school, I was becoming more and more speedy. I anticipated everything. I flicked the ashes off my cigarettes before there were any. When dancing along to the music, the music that was always there, the never-ending soundtrack to the movie, I would clap just a gnat's eyebrow ahead of the beat, which was really pissing off the gnat, because it was Nat King Gnat. (Unforgettable, that's what I am. Unforgettable, though I eat Spam). As though I was trying to hurry life along, to get it up to my speed. You can't stuff an entire baritone saxophone into your mouth. I was hyper-competent, hyper-aware. I knew exactly where everything was, getting to where it was going before it did. Unfortunately, I was also impatient with Paula. Helping her with her homework I tried to push her through it, to force her to understand everything, rather than letting her understand for herself. I found myself being short with her, something that never happened. At one point my impatience finally got to her, sweet and sensitive soul that she is, and very concerned about my approval. She began to cry. I felt awful, horrible, and apologized profusely. At last I got her to bed, compensating for my nastiness by reading to her at length from a favorite bedtime book and keeping her up much too late in the process.

Relieved that she was out of my hands I plunged headfirst into another night of non-stop activity. I was working on a Reptile Tape, a movie for the ears composed of hundreds of different bits of sound including snatches of conversations pulled from the radio, phrases lifted from commercials, music, sound effects, all thrown together into a sort of audio collage which moved at crazy angles creating the impression of a story. Were Reptile Tapes to be the key to my celebrity? They were indisputably original. The basis for a movie. Perhaps radio stations would buy them. They were brilliant, daring, wild. Certainly worth a million dollars to the right person. Just a matter of finding the person. Simple really. Success was so close

I could smell its perfume, I could feel its breath on the back of my neck. I worked on the Reptile Tape with headphones on, painstakingly selecting audio elements, at times a single word or sound, and laying them down carefully onto the master. I knew I needed to sleep because I had to get up early to take Paula to school, she was relying on me. Even so I forged ahead, inserting the sound of a creaking door, a sheep's bleat, an agonized human scream, a maniacal laugh, Richard Nixon explaining his innocence, James Brown begging Please, Please, Please, James Garner saying I've discovered that beef has magical properties, and on and on, a phantasmagorical Byzantine mosaic of sound crafted with agonized care one squizzified tile at a time. Baritone saxophones are made by people, kumquats occur naturally.

When I woke up I was lying face down on the living room floor, the headphones still on. I sat up and saw Paula watching cartoons on the couch. "I've been trying to wake you up for hours," she said. I panicked. I looked at my watch, it was nearly eleven. I went into a frenzy. Obviously sleep had caught me at last just before dawn. I fixed her breakfast in a hurry and took her to school as fast as I possibly could. Impatient with her again. I explained to her that I'd been working. It was true, I had been working, it wasn't an excuse, I wasn't lying to her, the Reptile Tapes were going to make me a fortune. We got to school and I took her to her class. She was clearly very embarrassed about being late for school and being escorted into her classroom by her father. Her teacher looked at me disapprovingly as only a teacher can. Screw her, Paula's mother and I pay her salary. Who is she to look askance at me, me, the Lizard King. Me, the man who put the zap in zaparoochie. But still, I was flushed red with embarrassment myself, however briefly. I had screwed up in front of Paula, I had let her down. Well, it wouldn't happen again. When I was a star, a celebrity, a snozzledrostopist, there would be a governess, Paula would be cared for to perfection. She had an unconventional father, it was a small price to pay for the harvest of bounty she was about to receive. I understood then that assuming the mantle of greatness gracefully while still minding to the minutiae of the commonplace world, the world of appointments, the world of slatch-heads, would require a certain amount of juggling. But I had the energy for it, and the powers of concentration. You don't need to carry a kumquat in a case with crushed velvet lining.

Chapter 22

What's So Funny?

Comedy is like landing a fighter jet on the deck of an aircraft carrier in the middle of the night. When it's done by those with no aptitude, experience, or timing, the results are hideous to behold and hard to clean up.

To be funny, you have to *be* funny. Any moron can learn a handful of nasty, racist, sexist jokes. Many do. A smaller number of morons can deliver them with that most elusive of comedy prerequisites, good timing. But to actually be funny you need to think funny. You need to see the world askew, you need a warped perspective. You need to be bent. That can't be faked and it can't be learned.

I don't remember exactly when I first realized I was funny, but I do know where I got it. My father was extremely funny. He was a masterful storyteller and entertainer. Also, he was a ruthless iconoclast, with no respect for anything. His madness too was a great contributor. Frequently he'd burst into song, making up absurdly comical lyrics as he went, sprinkling in hilarious fabricated words like mackooshla, glutch, and scradznitch. His perspective was uniquely his own, he skewered convention gleefully and pointed out absurdities at every available opportunity.

The more I viewed life as an outsider, the funnier I became. The more I refused to get serious about life, get ambitious, get greedy, get fiercely competitive, the funnier I became. Instead of engaging fully in the contests of life, I made fun of them. I was far too liberal to engage in cheap shots, no racial, religious, or sexist humor for me. I went for humor that ridiculed all of humanity. And I only told other people's jokes when I was desperate. Normally I created my own jokes. My favorite humor was situational, made up on the spot in response to something somebody said. People do enjoy this, but sometimes it has a way of pissing them off. If they want me to take them seriously, they don't need my constant wisecracks. Sometimes they feel like I'm ridiculing them directly.

Humor plays an absolutely essential role in my life. It's as important to me as music, it's a reason to live. At its best, it's a way for me to be happy and to make other people happy. It's a way to celebrate the fundamental lunacy and absurdity of life. It's a wonderful way to say outrageous things and get away with it. It's also a way to tell the truth and get away with it, and truth means everything to me.

These are the nobler aspects, as always, there are also murkier qualities.

Humor is a way for me to get attention and keep people at a safe distance at the same time. It's also a safe way to have power over other people. I tell a story, they're under my spell. I make them laugh when I want to, I control them, I control their responses. It's a benign power trip. Real power would be too frightening. It's also a very safe way for me to show off, I command the spotlight, but I can easily relinquish it whenever I want. As a comic I have complete control. If I bomb, it's my fault. If I kill, I get all the approbation. It's a safe way to be on stage, to face the judges, and come out a winner. And of course, it's a safe way to get approval.

But there's a deep hostility in humor. At times it's a way for me to build a wall around myself. If I dazzle you with funny smoke and mirrors, I distract you from my unwillingness to open up. I seem pleasant, because I'm funny and personable. In fact, I've wrapped my anti-social nature and my aggressive feelings in a velvet glove. This falsehood, this lie of comedy, penetrates many of my relationships with people.

In my normal life I make jokes constantly. I tell funny stories, I even have a few impressions up my sleeve. This can be a device to hide my power. By playing the buffoon, I tell people that I'm non-threatening. This, I hope, will keep them from being mean to me. As long as I'm funny, people don't have to take me seriously so I never provoke a showdown. Unfortunately, this technique paints me into a corner. When I do want people to take me seriously, they're disappointed that I'm not being funny. And that's a frustration, because under all the jokes is a very serious person, a person with strong beliefs and strong opinions. They do say that comics are the most serious people of all, the most serious, and the most damaged.

But, live by the rubber chicken and you die by the rubber chicken.

All comedy has its origins in pain, he said, dragging out the heavily bandaged remains of an observation first made in the time of Heraclitus. And life is pain. You laugh or you cry, it doesn't matter which. I've chosen laughter. It's been a way to make the pain tolerable. In my daily life, my humor is freewheeling and fun. When I was Manic, it roared like a chain saw. It was relentless, often cruel, and completely out of control. A massive edifice, keeping people out. It felt like my brain's way of amusing itself, I barely directed it at all. I was more the vehicle for, than the originator of, the humor. For much of the time I was every bit as surprised by my jokes as my audience.

My bewitched, bothered, and bewildered audience.

Well, that really wasn't very funny after all.

Chapter 23

Icy Spots

I drove directly to the closest of my acceptable spots, the Newport House. Spots equal watering holes. For a spot to make it onto my top ten list it has to be impeccable. My new credo is nothing but the best will do and even the best will only do until something better comes along. Quality is everything. Add quality to the list of things that are everything including timing, details, finding a good parking spot, having enough money on you to leave town at a moment's notice if you have to, and knowing all the lyrics to a song and not just the first verse. Less quantity, more quality. I'm not so concerned with the quantity of my audience as I am with the quality. If I perform for an audience of one, but that one is superb, I'm content. Small, intimate bars with faultless service and superb atmosphere have become my new environment. The natural habitat of a lounge lizard, a Komodo dragon with a tongue so long it could drive a skittish kitten right out of her mind. Icy spots before my eyes. And make no mistake, they're mine. I own them. For a spot to make my top ten list is quite an honor. How thrilled they must be! I have infallible instincts for what's best. Just another one of my remarkable talents, or gifts.

I selected my seat at the bar, it had to be the best seat, and settled. Like a dog which has to roam in circles a few times before lying down, I had to go through quite a ritual before settling in. Finding a place for my coat, stuffing my scarf in the sleeve. Determining the contents of my pockets, often an ambitious undertaking, and arranging them to my satisfaction. Finding a clean ashtray, not just an ashtray, a perfectly clean ashtray. Making certain that the bar area before me was clean and everything on it arranged to my satisfaction. Relentless devotion to order, to perfection, everything has to be just so, I'm a just so so and so. Then I could settle in, relax a bit, slack the pace of the blood that seems to race through me like river water through rapids. In a spot, I do a set. A set in the way a performer uses the word, an appearance. I'm not just another extippitox slatch-head sitting down at a bar. I'm the great Alistair McHarg, doing a set, at one of his spots. From the moment I make my entrance to my parting line, everyone knows I'm special. And if they don't know beforehand, I make sure to let them know. Every motion, every statement, carefully calculated for effect. These people were in the presence of a star. Al-is-star. In their eyes I was poised, theatrical, enjoying my free time, sardonically commenting on the passing spectacle. I looked the part. Zot. Snat. Rooch. Naparoopy.

I'm making a movie, and I'm the star. I've found all the best locations. The handsomest bartenders, the most beautiful bartenderettes. The most sultry music. You've got to be good to make it into this project. Lavish production value. For a bright smile and the sweet taste of sin chew Decadenteen. Billie Holiday's voice. The smoky flavor of cognac. The exquisite smoothness of Zelda's mink coat on my fingers. The marijuana's exotic aroma. The sight of a beautiful woman I'd never laid eyes on before. At last, I ordered my martini.

The room was small and uncrowded, a few groups of people at tables, and two businessmen eating lunch at the bar. A sedate place, part of why I like it. At my spots, I insist on being the center of attention. I stay away from busy places. The woman tending bar was sensational, my taste exactly. Tall, beautiful, incredible body, bright, nice. I would have slithered across the bar, slipped up her skirt, and insinuated my snazzjungulating self into her slish in a second if I'd thought I could've gotten away with it. And me newly in love, what a hound. But having her there, waiting on me, was a close second and I was content. Her name is Jane, I'd seen her there before. She's one of the reasons that the Newport House has made it onto my top ten list of spots. When I paid her for the drink I got back some very tatty, that's right he said tatty knowing full well that it sounds affected and loving it all the more for that reason, long live George Sanders and all other cads and rakes, one dollar bills in my change. I hate anything shabby and with so little money remaining I want the money I do have to be crisp. There's some very beat up currency circulating, bleached out, torn bills that should have been burned.

"Good Lord, Jane," I said, genuinely surprised, "look at these bills." Pause for effect, go for the gag which had popped into my head unsolicited, "This money looks like it's been laundered." Jane laughed. How I love you, you're quick. You're listening. You're with me. You can stay on the bus as long as you like. The two businessmen looked up from their lunches, they got it, they smiled. That's very good boys, have a biscuit. I pitched up a grapefruit and you caught it. You're clever enough to have survived round one. Let's see how well you do on the second round.

I was now standing by the bar, a stand up comic, they were sitting, slurping soup. I was decidedly not eating. "What a funny expression," I went on, "laundering money. You make money in a despicable, filthy way, selling weapons perhaps, and then you take your dirty money and make it clean again. I wonder what kind of laundry detergent you need to perform strange alchemy like that?" No longer Soupy Sales, now moving towards the Lenny Bruce, Dick Gregory school of comedy. The businessmen seemed to be wondering what the hell I was up to. I plowed forward with mock curiosity.

"Wow," I said, "I wonder what crack dealers use to wash *their* money. Tide wouldn't remove that kind of filth, not even Extra-Strength Tide. They probably have to use something special like that new stuff I saw at the market the other day, *Blood Of Our Savior Tide*." One of the businessmen dropped his spoon with a loud clank.

"Alistair," said Jane in an oh you naughty boy recriminating tone of voice, "cut it out. These people are trying to enjoy their lunch." The diners looked at her gratefully.

"Oh come on," I said back to her, "some people like to listen to music while they eat, others like to watch a comedian warm up." Because, I was just warming up. I do my real work downtown, at the Four Seasons. Get off quick, so they say. Sensing that I'd pushed just a bit too far, and not wanting to poison the well so that I couldn't return, I belted down the remains of the martini. Oh bless the intense, almost medicinal absoluteness of vodka. A gronzle right between the eyes. It didn't slow me down much but it did help to calm me, to sooth me.

"I'm off to the city," I said, mostly to Jane, assembling myself to depart with a flourish. I left a good tip, I always do, always taking care of the help. Taking care of the people who take care of me. No job, no money, no savings, no negotiable assets worth mentioning, no credit, no rich friends good for an easy touch, I still manage to always leave a good tip. Part habit, part genuine affection. Part fastidious attention to niggling details. I reached for Jane's hand, as if to shake it. She surrendered her hand and instead of shaking it, of course, I kissed it. All style, all flair, all flourish and all yours for the low low price of only your approval. Love me. Find me funny, charming, clever. Out the door he goes. Slam, zaparoopie. The set is over. Don't bother clapping. He's split. Absented himself. Deleted. Excused from the room. The cat's not part of the equation anymore.

Back in my car, all four windows rolled down exactly half way. Creates a very nice visual, another line bisecting the car on a vertical plane. Highly styled profiling for the '90s, don'tcha know. Appearance is so important. Making an appearance, little star. And appearances can be deceiving. I cruised down the avenue as cool and cocksure as an English rock star on an American tour. McHarg on his way to take the city by storm. Lock up your wife and hide your daughter. Blues lyrics will never let you down. Accused of murder, in the first degree, the judge's wife cried, set the poor boy free.

Gliding along easily, so far removed from the other occupants of the road, the drones on their way to appointments of unimaginable dullness. I looked around for a pilot car. Spots, sets, pilot cars. Rock stars, heads of state, gangsters, rarely drive alone, just in one car. There are two cars. The staff car and the pilot car. The pilot car leads the way, it contains the equipment, the drugs, the bodyguards. The staff car contains the celebrity and the chauffeur. What do you do? I'm a getaway driver for a rogue band of performance artists. There are many kinds of driving in this country and some of them are legal. So, in the course of my driving I frequently pick up a car which, without the driver knowing it, becomes my pilot car. Naturally it has to be a good one, a Jaguar XJ6 is my favorite and there are plenty, mostly driven by very well cared for middle-aged women. Good God. It ain't no drag, papa's got a brand new Jag. Free James Brown.

Or a Mercedes. But they're so common that it has to be a good one. It's binary. A good one, or nothing. It either is or it isn't. There are no gray areas any more. You're either on the bus or you're off. Rapanoochie. If you're part of the problem then go soak your head in a seven percent solution. Ratt zat noopie. So I picked up a pilot car, an Austin Healy 3000 as it turned out, a very good omen of how my luck was running. Omen, a four letter word if ever there was one. I followed it for as long as it was going my way, it was a cool, metallic blue gray. Wonderful car. A man driving. Badass pilot car, me in my mini-limo, the black Volvo four door sedan, windows half down in below freezing weather, staff car. My left leg had become stiff and I lifted myself out of the seat to stretch it, moving my bum slightly over to the right, that's right he said bum.

Stretching the leg out completely straight I found myself sitting in between the two seats, resting my rear on the handbrake assembly. That's right he said assembly leaving the joke there for you to put it together for yourself. Get it? This was a revelation. I was now sitting in the precise center of the car, driving along, raised above seat level. It gave me the most curious sensation of being in a small sailboat, sitting dead center in order to retain balance. I laughed out loud, this was marvelous. Simply naparoopie to the maxatopolis. What an entirely different perspective on driving. I wasn't driving down a road anymore, I was sailing down the road, steering wheel in my left hand. I laughed with explosive delight. The tired, old act of driving, as familiar and automatic as cheating on my income tax return, had become new. This was terrific. Then I wondered, if sitting in the middle was this fabulous, what would it feel like if I slipped all the way over to the passenger's seat?

I waited until I got a long, clear patch of road going downhill because I didn't want to worry about the pedals. By now the Healy was long gone but I didn't care, this was like discovering snozzling. Sure that I was in a safe spot I slipped all the way over to the passenger's seat, operating the steering wheel with my left hand and the accelerator with my left leg. Car driving normally, driver's seat empty, front passenger seat occupied. I've cracked up with laughter in my day but this just sent me over the top. It was all four of the Marx brothers rolled into one. Talk about your concept humor. Talk about your posmondillip snorch. Talk about your performance art. A car driving down the road with nobody in the driver's seat and a person sitting in the passenger's seat behaving as though there was nothing out of the ordinary going on? Oh please. I got a rush of pure pleasure, pure joy, pure delight. Divine madness. Inspired absurdity. Perfection. Without trying to I'd invented something new. I decided to name it Invisible Driving.

Like any intense rush, it was a little scary. And I certainly didn't want to get into an accident. So after just a few moments of this bliss I slipped back into the driver's seat and resumed business as usual. How ya' gonna keep 'em down on the farm after they've slipped through the slits in the scenery and discovered another reality? I parked by the Four Seasons as smug as a Christian holding four aces, as Twain nearly said when he wasn't too busy saying Man is the only animal that blushes and is the only animal with a need to.

Entering the Four Seasons was bliss on top of bliss. The doormen welcomed me in, I belonged there. I had a greeting for every staff member, reading their nameplates, remembering their names, calling them by their names, I'm always friendly to the staff. Because, after all, we're all in it together. They were working there and so was I. I proceeded into the Swan Lounge, the huge marvelous room which contains the small, faultless bar. Large windows looked out onto the tree lined parkway, the grand boulevard that connects the art museum to city hall. I took a perch. It was late afternoon, the room was roughly half full. I was alone at the bar. The bartender was Matthew, an impossibly handsome black man with a keen wit and a winning smile. Matthew is on the bus. Pleasant, witty, crisply professional, he is a favorite audience of mine because he has style, mind and soul. Astounding how being an outsider develops character in a person, gives that person depth. Compassion. And no matter how handsome Matthew is, he is still a black man in a white culture. And gay, big surprise there. If Matthew was any more gay he would be Jean Genet. Or perhaps, Paul Verlaine, looking for the end of the Rimbaud. Brings to mind what Oscar Wilde said when he was sitting in a hotel lobby with a book in his hand and a friend told him it was time to leave, wait, just let me get to the bottom of this page. But folks.

What makes Matthew great above the other qualities is that he inhabits these two oppressed minority groups without any self-righteous bitterness. He's sarcastic, he's caustic, oh all right I'll say it, he's acerbic, but he doesn't play the victim. (The victim was played by a mysterious Norwegian named Raoul sent over by Central Casting). He looks at the world with a jaundiced eye, a sharp eye, but he doesn't behave as though it has been constructed merely to make him miserable. He made me a martini, after just a few encounters he already knew my drink and exactly how I liked it prepared. Oh Lord the difference between the merely competent and the excellent. I settled in, more relaxed than I had been for a long time. I was at home. No appointments. Not trying to pick up a girl. No objectives other than to keep from going totally nazzbat.

I fished through my pockets, using a daredevil spinner with three-prong barbed hooks because I like to live dangerously, and found a nail file. What luck. And there, in front of God and all the world, I sat and methodically sanded the burrs off of my nails. As though I was the most bored Sultan in the world, without a single problem to concern me, passing the time idly with a little bit of personal grooming. It was an extremely soothing activity. Chewed off, raggedy nails scratch a woman's skin, spoiling a romantic mood. It's good policy to keep those nails and fingertips free of offensive obtrusions. Hence the nail file. Now I'm not doing comedy, I'm merely doing performance art. Waiting for the room to fill up. Glancing out the windows, always observing, relentlessly aware, hyper-awareness, can't switch it off, analyzing, evaluating, cataloging.

Outside the great windows, in the bitter cold, I watched three beggars. They're holding coffee cups, going up to the cars in line waiting for the light to change, and tapping on the windows. Sometimes they got change, sometimes they were ignored. Incredible collections of clothing these men wear. Ragged sweaters on top of other ragged sweaters, coats on top of coats, the inevitable ski cap with the logo of a sports team, all so horribly filthy as to be almost completely colorless, a sort of uniform gray. I watched them working the line of cars light after light after light. The determination of cockroaches. The resilience of ants which have had their nest kicked in.

"You know one of my favorite things about the Four Seasons," I said to Matthew. He encouraged me to continue. "You can see people from both ends of the social scale without even turning your head. Look at those poor bastards out there, begging just to stay alive, while the people in here drink fifty-year-old cognac and dine on quail's eggs."

He nodded in agreement. He's a sophisticate and a mensch, what a wonderfully special combination.

"Look at these goddamned people," I went on, sweeping a manicured hand around the room for emphasis, indicating the collection of fops, poseurs, moguls, movers and shakers, tycoons, dealmakers and debutantes that composed a considerable percentage of the room's inhabitants, "biting and clawing their way to the top."

Matthew smiled broadly. "Yes, I know," he responded, lisp blazing, responding quickly I threw some water on the lisp and put it out, "and the sad thing is, after they've sold their souls, most of them will only have clawed their way to the middle."

I laughed heartily at this one, secure that I had spent my last days in the middle. I was headed for the top, hell, I was already there. Because to really be on top, you had to understand it all. You had to understand the suffering of the meanest, most deprived creatures and the ecstasy of the most perfectly fulfilled. Too much range for most people to handle. But I'm as big as Alaska, sufficiently grand to contain even the most elemental contradictions.

I walked from the bar over to a bank of payphones and made a deposit, they were giving away free toasters if you opened an account. With the blissful contentment of a man with a large appetite about to sit down to a gourmet dinner, I called Claire at work. I arranged to pick her up and give her a ride home. We would find something to eat, she said. Work at the Four Seasons, play at Claire's. The elements of my new life were falling beautifully into place like geometric pieces of a child's puzzle. Since I never slept or ate I didn't have to worry about those elements. I couldn't wait to go driving again, Invisible Driving, more concept humor to go. So what'll it be bub? Oh, I'll have one concept humor to go, please, hold the logic. I'm doing everything possible to attract fame, and the success that will come with it. We're down to cases now, just details to work out. When the Goddess Fortune arrives and taps me on the shoulder, asking me politely to put my autograph on a contract, I know that my reaction will be simply, what took you so long?

Chapter 24

Trash

I'm constantly picking things up. Not valuable things. Souvenirs. Things that capture my attention. Documenting where I've been. Sometimes things just appeal to me and I tuck them into my pockets. Periodically I empty my pockets onto a periodic table, a most extraordinary experience, if elementary. The damndest things show up. Of course, matches from my favorite spots, the swankest watering holes in Philadelphia. The Four Seasons. The Bellevue. The Barclay. The Rittenhouse. I especially like hotels. Then there are the small restaurants, I'm building up quite a tour. This is my circuit, it's short, and highly charged. Get it? I've put myself on a talk show circuit, performing at the best restaurants and hotels in the area. I've thrust myself into the spotlight, entertaining daily, nightly, constantly.

Your trash is my art. Wire has begun to attract my eye, there's a lot of it lying on the street, especially around construction sites. I pick it up and start working it with my hands, usually without breaking my stride, when I do break my stride I have to put it into a cast of thousands. I make elaborate snake sculptures out of the pieces. The brightly colored plastic coatings of electrical wire are cheerful. The beauty of copper wire is irresistible. Phone wire makes excellent braid. Silver wire, the kind that holds together wooden packing crates, looks expensive. Working the wire gives me something to do with my hands besides smoking. The snake sculptures are proliferating.

My pockets are full of snakes and my fingertips are in ribbons with little wire cuts. I have peaceful snakes, coiled in repose. I have mean cobras with arched backs, standing tall and ready to strike, for higher wages, of sin. (Wow, that was a good one, even for me). How do I come up with this stuff? I was always funny, but I never used to be this funny.

I have elegant, long snakes whose bodies sway back and forth like a windy road. Not a *windy* road, a *windy* road. Fearing that they might multiply in my pockets I leave them in strategic locations. Unsigned. Little objets d'art which I hope will hit the bull's eye. Something unexpected. To be found by someone who would say, "What the hell is this?" or "isn't that pretty" or, dread the thought, nothing at all. I have a heart as big as all Manhattan, leaving my little wire reptiles to delight the multitudes. Art into life, make my life my art, performance art.

Moving things from one pocket to another, throwing things out and accumulating new things, is a constant process. It's as though my hands have a life of their own. At any given moment I'm carrying four or five lighters, for the constant cigarettes and joints, and of course, to light the cigarettes of women, God what a gentleman I am. The very picture of a gentleman. Deferential and accommodating to women, witty, interested in them. Admiring. Finding things in my pockets. The matches from the swank spots. Useful for showing that I know where the best spots are. Useful as giveaways. "By the way, if you want to try another really sweet spot, here." Then press the selected matchbook into the palm. Our little secret amulet. She then knows that it's good, and that she can find me there too. Generous. Sharing my knowledge of what is good. An intense desire to please, entirely selfless. I find pleasure in pleasing others.

The humor comes from this. What better thing to give a person than a laugh, even if it is hard to wrap. Finding things in my pockets. Bonus points. Bonus points are washers. I see them on the street, looking like little lost zeros. If I see an interesting one, particularly large or small or perfectly formed, I pick it up and pocket it. I have plastic ones that are brightly colored and metal ones that weigh me down. If someone does or says something that impresses me, if somebody connects with a joke or somehow demonstrates brain activity, I award a bonus point. The gesture is usually received with bemused appreciation. Who is this guy with the pockets that never end? Women are so accustomed to being hit on by conventional guys at bars in conventional ways that something odd can be disarming. Especially if the guy is only looking for an appreciative audience, not to get laid. Not that I only give them out to women. Bartenders, especially at the tonier spots, tend to be a world-weary, wise, sarcastic lot, well cast for my brand of humor. I've assigned several bonus points to bartenders. I've skipped a few on the blackened Delaware River too during the darkest hours of the night as I wondered if this was all some sort of dream run amuck.

My pockets have enough business cards to start three rolodexes. Cards with women's names and phone numbers scribbled on the back. Cards of musicians. Cards from limousine companies, restaurants, bars, strangers I've met at bars. I have cards of magicians, mimes, (mimes need business cards more than the average professional and a mime is a terrible thing to waste), florists, erotic lingerie vendors, others, everything you'd need to start a nightclub, an escort service, a limousine company, or a troupe of rogue performance artists. The cards too keep changing, like a river passing through my pockets, that's it, that's why I'm always fishing in my pockets, at last I've figured it out. Always upgrading, only the best will do. Joints, yes there are always joints and roaches floating around in my pockets. I've made some wonderful roach clips out of found wire too. Packs of cigarettes, naturally. Photographs. Bits and pieces I intend to use in collages. Ah, one day, I will retire to the country and do only collage, unless of course I exhaust the medium, and break her crystal ball, and graduate from collage. But not today. Photographs torn from magazines. Receipts from money access machines, automatic tellers, like me, an automatic truth teller. I'm searching the universe for clues to explain my next move. The one thing that my pockets are free of is money. But there is value. Surely knowing where all the best spots are is a valuable knowledge. But not something I can convert to cash. Not without becoming a pimp, or an escort. And I haven't fallen to that. Sex is for pleasure, so marvelous that it shouldn't be ruined by money. If you want to know what you should be doing for a living, look to the things you do for free. Those are the things you love the best. And I'm living for a living, pushing the envelope of discovery.

Chapter 25

Daddy, Where Does Art Come From?

One of my professors in graduate school told me one day that he was, "Coming down with a poem." How lovely when a thought is perfectly expressed. I've been writing poems practically my whole life and I've always felt that they were writing me more than I was writing them. Or, at the very least, that I was simply a vehicle to get them produced, a courier. They originated elsewhere, from an unknown source.

In the same sense that a microbiologist, himself composed of cells, might be studying cells not because he wants to, but because cells need a way to learn more about themselves.

Poetry, music, collage, photography. The creative force has pushed me into various venues. It's a drive as basic to me as survival itself and it demands expression. When it summons, I obey. When it doesn't, I don't try to coax it.

As a young man, having completed a poem, I would look in wonder at the strong emotions, the way the phrases were turned. It was as if someone else had written it. In my more spiritual moments I believed that this must be the work of God, that I was just a tool of God, that God was directing my hand. I needed a profound explanation because it was so clearly not the work of my conscious mind.

For one thing, I didn't think I was technically good enough to have produced it. For another, I didn't believe that I was spiritually deep enough to have pulled it off. Most important, I didn't feel that I had the emotional freight to generate that kind of material. It was actually a little bit frightening. I had to admit I'd done it, but I didn't understand how I could have.

For the most part my poetry was very cerebral and serious. My favorite themes were death, God, heaven, the transcendent beauty of nature, transformation, and redemption. Sometimes my skeptical mind stopped me from attributing these tiny outbursts of art to God. On those occasions I felt connected to something else, something unknowable, something larger than myself that wasn't God. A muse, perhaps, the music of the spheres, some universal force. At the very least they made me realize that there were mysterious things going on inside of me. Things I didn't even know about. They surfaced when they wanted to surface. It was strange, spooky, and exciting. Because it mastered me and not vice versa, I could revel in it and still maintain complete humility.

I grew accustomed to the idea that I had a wild, raw power over which I had no control. The power to create.

My creative life seemed to run in waves, gradual cycles. For months I would very nearly vegetate. Then I would go into short periods of intense activity. In retrospect I realize that these might have been "hypomanic" cycles, that in fact I might have been operating this way all my life. Long periods of mild depression interrupted by short bursts of Manic energy and Manic creativity. Manic, but not so intense or bizarre that anybody would find them disturbing. Not so extreme that the levels of creativity would be baffling to others.

In the times of true Mania, the secret wellspring of my creative energy had a going-out-of-business, lost-our-lease, everything-must-go, garage-sale-of-the-mind sale. Normally dark and mysterious, meting out its magic in dribs and drabs, it tore down the curtains, slapped back the shutters, and opened itself up for all the world to see. The level of creativity was stunning, but there was no judgement.

I now know why creative artists who are Manic Depressive often refuse help. They're so exhilarated in their highs that they can't imagine giving them up. They'll even accept the pain, the crash, the depression as a reasonable price for the unfettered creativity and energy. It's a strategy I've decided against, but I do understand it.

When I was Manic, I was in constant touch with that inner well. Because all the governing layers of my brain were shut down, there was nothing separating me from the force itself. It wasn't that I created wonderful art, I was too out of control to be productive in any meaningful way. It was far more thrilling than that.

I existed in art. Every fiber of my being was fixed in a state of constant creativity. Constant inventiveness. Constant newness. Every idea in the attic was dusted off and slammed full-force onto the table for consideration. New ideas spewed forth like lava from a volcano. Weird combinations of ideas appeared out of nowhere. The sheer volume of my mind's productivity overwhelms me to this day. It was like a holy revelation, a moment of grace that went on for months.

I knew at last the source of the words, the images, the feelings which had been inhabiting my poems for decades. That unchartable landscape within, where angel wings disturb the dust and the infinite intersects with the temporal. I heard the roar. I saw it in all of its sanctified, uncivilized splendor.

My visionary, mad, and mystical soul.

Chapter 26

Spike

Scrooch. Snat. Zeep. Babarooby. The days of January melt together into the seamless scenery of sets in spots, Invisible Driving, walking the streets of downtown Philadelphia as though I'm late for a TV appearance, steamy evenings and weekends of squilching with Claire, and visits with Paula. Never go near my house except to change clothes. Any sleeping I do, precious little, I do in post-snozzle rapture tangled in Claire's arms. Stopped checking my mailbox altogether, why bother, that's the past. Gave Claire's phone number to Sarah, explaining this is where I spend most of my time. She's relieved. Been trying to call my number, she should know I've changed my number, my new number is Number One, and getting a recording saying there's trouble with the line. I'm not having any trouble with *my* lines, "Come apart here often?" Obviously they cut off my phone and I didn't even feel a thing. No problem, I'll use Claire's number for the public. Later I'll get my own phone at Claire's with a number so unlisted even I won't write it down. In keeping with my new star status natch.

Sarah's getting oochie about Paula visiting me in the wilds of West Philly. Told her that visits would be at my place only. Paula suffers as a result. I can't stand being in my old place a second longer than I have to. Going on two months without paying rent. Being there reminds me of my old life, the life I'm leaving behind. Wonder about moving my things to Claire's. Workable idea except there's so little room on the third floor if

a gnat breaks wind up there he'll blow out a window. No worry.
I'll make the place over. Transform it into the palace it could be,
Taj McHarg. Convince Sarah it's a fine place for Paula to visit.
It'll take some doing but Claire likes my decorating ideas and
God knows I have the energy.

My second best spot is the Bellevue, the grand dame
of Philadelphia's hotels, best remembered for the infamous
Legionnaire's disease debacle. Completely restored and
resplendent yes he said resplendent when a slatch-head would
have said it's, like, ya' know, real pretty, with the swankest shops
including Gucci's, Ralph Lauren, and my favorite, Dunhill, it's
arguably the most opulent hotel in Philadelphia. Operated by
Cunnard it exudes a world-class atmosphere that is tainted by
stuffiness and frou-frou decor. Still, on the top floor it affords a
sensational view and I can afford the view too though not much
more, across historic Philadelphia, across the Delaware River, a
cross I can't bear much longer, far off into the distance. In fact
one is merely gazing across New Jersey, the social equivalent
of anti-matter, but the lights of New Jersey blink just as
romantically at night as do the lights of Istanbul if one forgets
what one is looking at and lets one's imagination fly freely and I
don't need to let my imagination fly anymore I *am* imagination.

The bar on the top floor is somebody's idea of what a library
in an English castle would look like, complete with banks of
leather bound books, busts of Greek philosophers and a marble
chess set which, God forbid anybody should actually use. The
books too are presumably equally off limits. I've been tempted
in fact to see if, like Gatsby's, they are actually real. I'll wager
they are and also, like Gatsby's, simply there for affect. But the
atmosphere is elegant and soothing, the help beautifully attired
and attractive, and it fits me like a tailored shirt. An opulent,
world-class elegance that raises me high above petty concerns
like phone bills and car payments.

One evening not long ago I was sitting at the bar at the
Bellevue, trying to stop shaking, stop sweating, being waited on
by a female bartender I especially like. A short, slightly tough

young woman with closely cropped blond hair. Crisp demeanor.
Demean her, why, I hardly know her. But folks. Quick wit. Wiry
frame. Very businesslike. We were talking about dancing and
she told me that she didn't dance. Then she corrected herself,
using a pair of corrective dance slippers, and said with sly
mischievousness that the only dancing she did was behind bars.
She even gave me a tantalizing simulation, laughing to herself. A
caged cat, God, I could feel the heat. But I was merely minding
my own business, sorting through the contents of my pockets.
The man with the endless pockets.

Cigarette lighters, matchbooks from my spots, bonus
points, leaflets with phrases I intend to use later in collages, bits
of wire, the odd spoon, and, quite incredibly, a full sized railroad
spike. I'd picked it up earlier that day, wandering along railroad
tracks by the Schuylkill River. It looked like a stylized capital
letter T, with a marvelous patina. Old, rusted, pockmarked
with wear and weather, it had been irresistible to me. Unlike
some things I pick up I had no idea of what I would do with it.
I just found it marvelous, (oh stop calling me marvelous, you're
embarrassing me), and I had to have it. It had so much character,
I'm developing a sculptor's eye for form. Add sculpture to the
list of things I'll be doing successfully in the near future. It
weighed a hell of a lot but I was determined to add it to my
increasingly far-reaching collection of found objects d'art. I laid
it on the barstool beside me.

When the firm and love me tender bartenderette asked
me for my drink I ordered my usual martini with a glass of
water on the side, a frequent request. I was sweating a lot and
losing water. The vodka only served to dehydrate me more so
I often got water on the side. Almost before I put in my order
it was in front of me. Clear martini in a clear martini glass, a
saucy, wide open V balancing on top of a capital I. Clear, pure
water with ice cubes in a tall, clear, cylindrical glass. Pure and
simple, no frills. Both glasses sat before me, sweating, just like
me. Then, another tiny brain snorch, a little electronic bridge
between two cells. I started to laugh but then stifled it. When
the bartender was looking away I placed the spike carefully

inside the tall water glass. I sipped some of the martini. When she shifted her attention back in my direction I hailed her with a theatrical mock formality, "Miss." She looked at me. "Excuse me, Miss," I went on, in a tone of stilted seriousness, a tone of conspiratorial concern, a tone of tazmopulated squizzification, eyes moving her eyes towards the clear cylinder containing the offending piece of railroad memorabilia, "I believe someone has spiked my drink."

She looked at it and completely broke up, her downtown hipster cool kittyness temporarily blown out.

"Oh my God," she said, "I've never seen that done." Why, indeed, would anyone but amazing me do it? She laughed with real enthusiasm, delighting me. I began to laugh too, reveling in the sheer absurdity of it. The perfect weapon to puncture the pompous balloon upon which floats the Bellevue.

"Can I keep this?" she asked. "I want to show it to the others." I told her of course she could, thrilled to be memorable. I finished the martini and paid, leaving her a generous tip. I bade her a very fond adieu as I feigned interest in a very bad fondue, positively beaming at the highlight, get it, celebrating the lapse of appropriateness we'd enjoyed together. Out the door he goes. Without an explanation. Rabazibby. Who is that guy and why does he do it? Zot. Root. Snootch. Snazzmatic. Existing only in your memory.

Chapter 27

Our National Anthem

There's something disturbing about a man walking down a busy city sidewalk whistling the national anthem. (Of course there's also something disturbing about a man sucking the intestines out of a live armadillo but that's not the point right now). Especially if he looks like just another stockbroker except that he's wearing a National Rifle Association tractor cap. And he's whistling the Jimi Hendrix version.

While the U.S. is a great country, and it is a great country, although certainly not nearly as great as everyone seems to think it is, and certainly not the greatest country in the world as so many slatch-heads are fond of saying with the annoyingly mindless regularity of trained parrots, it has a really lousy national anthem. Even the best singers are barely able to sing it at all, much less make it enjoyable to listen to. And everybody forgets the words. Why? Because the lyrics are awful. A rambling, incoherent paean, to a flag of all things, a musically ghastly monstrosity which begins with a question and ends with a question and in between provides very little in the way of answers, and a glorification of war. If our elected officials had any chops at all, that means balls that means cheese that means moxie that means backbone, (does it need to be pointed out that they don't, apparently I think it does because I have), they'd change the national anthem to America The Beautiful and be done with it. In the meantime, we're stuck with this turkey.

I've heard a variety of brilliant singers attempt this high wire act and every time I just couldn't wait for it to be over. Even the redoubtable Ray Georgia On My Mind Hit The Road Jack You Don't Know Me Drown In My Own Tears Charles can't turn it into music. But there's one version that I love, that's the version by Jimi Hendrix. He had the wit not to try to sing it but just played it on the guitar in his snazzblaster, squizzslushing, squatchatopolis electrotectonic style. The national anthem performed by an orchestra consisting of three band saws cutting steel, a jackhammer, seven air raid sirens, a machine gun, and an electrical power station going up in flames. Now that's entertainment. Hendrix performed his version during the height of the Vietnam bloodbath and the protest against it. For me, his rendition soulfully embodied all the anguish of that war, war in general, and the torment of a country tattered and torn. For the first time I could see the rocket's red glare, I could feel the bombs bursting in air. I got the idea. It registered with me way down in the kitchen, way down in the chitlins.

Whistling the Hendrix version of the national anthem took breath but if there's one thing I had it was energy. It tested my abilities as a whistler too. But it was worth it. By disturbing others, unsettling them, by enlarging the scope of their blindingly bland day with a dazzling sprinkling of my own unique brand of snerchiness, I was making an important contribution. In the sense that art, when it's at its best, causes people to see things in new ways. Yes it delights, yes it pleases, hit me one time again James Brown, it Pleases Pleases Pleases, as I was determined to please please please, but also it challenges everything you take as given by allowing you to enter something differently. Hence my constant irreverence. Not in an attempt to ridicule, but in an attempt to unsettle convention. Unfortunately there were no conventions in town at the time. To do the thing that others only think about doing.

I presented an intimidating front. Tall, big, severe features, walking faster than most people run, I was not a guy a sane person would pick a fight with. And topped off with a National Rifle

Association tractor cap I was both inexplicable and threatening. The cap was an inside joke to amuse myself. I'd found it. I'm anti-gun but pro-murder. My belief is that if people want to kill each other they should be encouraged as much as possible and given every opportunity to do so. In all human logic there seems to be an article of faith, an underlying assumption, that people are somehow intrinsically worthwhile, useful, desirable, and needed. Who the hell ever proved this point? I can't imagine finding many animals who'd agree with it except for some effete lap poodles. Looking at what humankind has done to the earth during its relatively short period of suzerainty leads one to the only reasonable conclusion which is that Man is some sort of global plague, some dreadful evolutionary mistake run amuck.

However, murder is a serious act and should not be entered into lightly or impulsively, as happens so frequently with guns, the Saturday night fight over which TV show to watch which ends tragically in gunplay sort of scene. If a person is going to kill another person, it should be done deliberately, and with bare hands. If you had to look into the eyes of the person you were killing, you'd think more about the significance of your act. Handguns make murder cheap. There's no place for handguns in a civilized society. The NRA's defense of handguns is a national badge of shame. Wearing the hat was funny because it was absurd. But, to the casual observer walking the crowded sidewalks of downtown Philadelphia during the lunch rush, I was a guy conservatively dressed except for a detail which belied everything else. Whistling at full voltage. But what is he whistling? Jesus it sounds like the, the national anthem, but what's that buzzing sound? How does he make that buzzing sound? By snizzling inside, by burning inside like Jimi's burning guitar, by squazzling and snorching in ways that you'll never know, in ways you could not even spell. Because I've got IT, the magic. I've gone zatchmatic and now everyone knows. Out the door, out the door, out the door he goes.

Chapter 28

I'm A Professional, Don't Try This At Home

In late August of 1970, my fellow Haverfordians were packing up their bathing suits, closing up all those houses on the Cape, and heading back to resume the collegiate life. I was sitting in a prison cell in West Germany, suffering from amoebic dysentery. Weak from having lost thirty pounds in two months. Addled from having been stoned on powerful hashish for the entire summer. Certain that I'd been disowned by my parents.

What I didn't realize was that things were about to get even worse. I was about to struggle through my first Manic episode.

For people in the polite world, one step off the path is a catastrophe. For the mentally ill, (my fellow travelers), it's a lot different. Prison, asylums, police, doctors, mood drugs, sleeping in cars, the occasional beating, it's just not a big deal. It goes with the territory. Polite people imagine it much differently than what it's really like. It's not the end of the world. Embarrassment about such things is a luxury that's way too expensive for us. We have more basic concerns.

Twenty-five years later, I still don't know what the hell I was thinking. It was the stupidest thing I've ever done in my life. The most reckless. The most hurtful. I wish my mother were still alive so I could apologize to her all over again. I know I scared her half out of her wits.

All I can offer is that I was a rebellious kid with a famous father. I wanted to do something outrageous, I was thrill-seeking. Most stupid of all, I thought I could get away with anything.

Together with a friend from college I set out upon the hashish trail. From Italy to Greece, Turkey, Iran, a lot of time in Afghanistan, Pakistan, and then back West. In Afghanistan I bought two kilos of extremely good hashish, so black and fresh that it bent like road tar. Trips to an opium den, cocaine bought legally in a drug store, acid at the Green Hotel in Kabul, the journey was graduate level research in the effects of drugs on the brain.

So began the smuggling. The first country was Iran where the penalty for drug possession, especially for smuggling purposes, was death. Then Turkey, Greece, Albania, Yugoslavia, Austria. Many borders crossed, I did get away with it for a while. But my luck ran out at the border separating Austria and West Germany. I told the police my friend knew nothing about it and he was sent on his way.

Even in my daring crime spree I was small potatoes, two kilos for God's sake, barely enough to whet the whistle of a place like Haverford. Certainly not enough to make it worth risking my life. But there was no rhyme or reason to any of it, it was just stupid self-indulgence and self-destruction.

For ten days I sat in a solitary cell, entertaining abandonment fantasies, picturing myself a waif wandering about Europe, wasting away in menial jobs. Then the sound of jailer's keys and I was in a lawyer's Mercedes and then a yellow Lufthansa and then JFK. My father's friends in the State Department had made it all happen like magic. The jaded customs official looked at the pages of my passport with disbelief, turning them back and forth over and over, making a clucking sound with his tongue.

I could have easily cleaned the toxins out of my system. I could have handled the stigma. What I wasn't prepared for was facing my parents. I wasn't ready for the shame, the guilt. Knowing I'd caused them such pain for no good reason. So, my mind performed that Manic magic. It denied the reality of my responsibility. It went off.

The classic symptoms appeared. No sleep. Constant motion. Constant talking. Grandiose delusions, this time taking the form of a mystic holy man from the East railing against the stench of Western decay. I had been to the desert, I knew the answers.

I transformed a beautiful Danish coffee table my parents had given me into a major work of art, The Ash-Heap of History, using a bizarre collection of artifacts, and set the damn thing on fire. That's what did it. My parents took me to a psychiatrist who loaded me down with Thorazine. I felt like I'd been shot with an elephant gun. I barely had enough energy to break wind. However, it did the trick, it killed the high. I recovered enough to return to college, to the complete amazement of everybody. I went on to graduate with honors.

The psychiatrist did not diagnose me as Manic Depressive. In time we all forgot about it. There were other things to think about. My father's career was skyrocketing. My mother's illness was getting much more serious. We reasoned that it was just an emotional disturbance, a freakish aberration.

It would have been so nice if I'd gotten off that easily.

Chapter 29

The Fifth Season

One evening I was whiling away the hours at the bar in the Four Seasons, on my best behavior, on my favorite stool, on and on and on and on, listening to a man in a tuxedo playing the most superb lounge jazz. The room was roughly half full, that's right he said half full, not half empty, with a characteristic assortment of exquisitely dressed magnates, dealmakers, bon vivants, ne'er do wells, fops, dandies, matrons, courtesans and cunning call girls. The lounge lizard smiles, surrounded by cold blooded compatriots. Occasionally swapping caustic comments, some were so caustic we had to wear rubber gloves, with Peter, my other favorite bartender, but mostly listening to the music. I was alone at the bar except for a natty, middle-aged gentleman who was staring ahead into space. He had the look of a stranded businessman, which was irritating the stranded businessman who demanded his look back in anger, a typical guest, pouring off some time in between appointments.

The music was excellent, jazz standards from the Ellington school, which happened to be right down the street, adjacent to Thelonius Monk University, executed with both precision and feeling. It began to annoy me that the people inhabiting the room seemed completely unaware of the piano player. Yes I know it's background music and yes I know this is not a concert and yes I know unobtrusiveness is part of the point but the self-absorbed way these people ignored him, as though he was some sort of modern day android player piano pissed me off. After each song I felt the urge to clap, to give credit where credit was so clearly due, but nobody else did and I didn't want to draw any more attention to myself than I already did. When he ended his set he came over to the bar for a soda and I told him how much I enjoyed his performance. I named the tunes he played, a pointless exercise since they already had names, their composers, and we chatted about our favorite renditions of the numbers in question. He figured me for a music lover and got into it, as did the other man at the bar who was by now listening quite intently. The table was set.

"Yeah," I said, "I'm really sorry I didn't clap. I wanted to, you were playing so well, but then I saw the sign."

What had been an appreciative smile on his face twisted into a look of confusion. "What sign?" he responded.

"The sign right behind your head," I went on, "it kind of sets the tone in this place. You know, the one that says 'No Loud Ties, No Thinking, No Clapping.'"

He smiled a generous, genuine smile. Every artist, no matter how coolly professional he or she might be, is warmed by an audience that is both educated and appreciative. But I was pushing it just a bit further. I was angry on his behalf for the insensitivity shown by this crowd. Pearls before self-absorbed swine with designer rings through their noses. The ones who can afford to listen to the music don't have the taste, interest, or depth to appreciate it. Ironies were being laid upon ironies like layers of lacquer on a Chinese box. Within the absurdity of life lies the hope.

Having built an audience of two I decided to play out my hand. I began to assemble my things, getting ready to leave. I looked at the bill and then looked at Peter. One never speaks of money in the Four Seasons, it's an if you have to ask you can't afford it kind of place. So many taboos to be broken, so little time. With a face as deadpan as Buster Keaton's I asked, in a tone of voice which suggested that it was my first time there, "Excuse me, do you accept stolen credit cards?"

Peter, who is as fast on his feet as Cassius Clay used to be, responded dryly with that precise Four Seasons demeanor which bespeaks impeccable service, "Of course."

I made quite a play of hunting through my pockets, though only a one-act play. Ah ha! No longer fishing, now hunting. Wonder if there's a fox in there.

"How about bad checks?"

Peter never batted an eye, (of course he never batted over two-fifty either but I didn't have the heart to trade him), "With proper I D."

At last I pulled out my wallet and handed him a twenty. He went to the register to ring me up. By now the piano player and the patron were completely ours. "Oh," I piped up, "and could I have my change in counterfeit threes, please?" That got 'em. It's all a show, leave 'em laughing when you go.

I made my exit from The Four Seasons, a passerby might have thought I was the favorite son on his way to war. I said goodbye to everyone, always calling them by name, working my way out the door. Who knows what they thought? By now I was there so much they surely must have imagined I was a guest, more than a guest, that I had taken up residence there. Like an actor in town to make a movie, setting up shop. I walked into the night air with long, confident strides, a man on top of the world. How odd, I feel most at home amid this opulence and yet I identify most strongly with outsiders, the disenfranchised. Into which demographic pigeonhole do I fit? Perhaps there isn't one, perhaps that's my real brilliance, that I can't be categorized. I can tune in all the frequencies. An amazing gift, one which I'm bound by duty-free shopping to share.

I retrieved my car and crawled along the streets towards Claire's, toying with invisibility. Now it's a car being driven at night by a man wearing sunglasses. Now it's a car with no driver and a man in the passenger seat. These stunts are not easy at night, especially in city traffic, but I go to the mat for my audience. I parked my car in front of Claire's house. I rang the bell. No answer. Claire told me once that she never answered the door if she wasn't expecting anybody. Christ, she really ought to have a drawbridge in front of this place, stock a moat with that most superb of all reptiles, the alligator, and do it right, I thought. I still didn't have keys. Time to talk to Claire about a set of keys, time to make it official. Finally Prince Wilson answered the door. Prince Wilson never says hello or what's happening, his universal greeting is, "Peace." But with that barrel-chested deep voice, unsmiling face, and intimidating demeanor, it sounds like he means, "War." He let me in, eyed me suspiciously, two territorial males competing for dominance, locked the door behind me, and I ascended the stairs of the castle showing my ass-end to Prince Wilson the fool of the castle, up above street level, up above the level of the common people, to the third floor, where the King and Queen live.

Claire was in her workroom, a misnomer because while there was work there was no room. She was concentrating intently on a painting which showed a pair of female buttocks covered by the filmiest, transparent panties. They were wrapped in plastic and displayed on a red tray as though they were pork chops for sale in the meat section of a supermarket. On the right one was a huge, red circular seal which said, "USDA Approved." I looked at it, shocked by the anger.

"For the radical feminists, I assume?" was all I could offer.

She put down her brush and stepped back, looking at it. "Sometimes it feels good to be angry," she said, and drew me out of the workroom, using charcoal and a sketch pad, and into the bedroom. In the course of the snozzling which followed we discussed our domestic arrangement. What did she think of letting me have my own keys? The keys symbolized everything, they would make it official. And it would mean so much to me, I could let go of my place and the financial worries that went with it. She was scared. Claire's not impulsive, she thinks long and hard about things.

"I've been alone for a long time, I'm used to living my own way." That was the understatement of the century. She had a point but in my mind I was already redesigning the place completely, with total abandon taking control, throwing out Prince Wilson and Ultraviolet, cleaning the place from top to bottom, painting it, throwing out ninety percent of the shit Claire had packed the place with, transforming it into the Fifth Season. At last she said all right, I could have keys. We would try the experiment of living together. No promises no demands. Just mutual respect. I was in. My beachhead, (does the ocean give beach head?), in the city. My new headquarters, (it takes a lot of quarters to afford head). No money had changed hands and yet miraculously I had a house. God, I really am unbelievable. I can do anything. Pozmondillip. My campaign to conquer the city was in full swing.

Claire told me that Sarah had called for me. Oh how I love the big time, my kitten to take my phone messages while I perform at the Four Seasons, what a life. I called Sarah. When she answered I smelled trouble, her tone of voice was sour. Usually we get along very well, my ex-wife and I, so I was not encouraged. We knocked the polite conversation tennis ball across the net a few times, starting with love and ending with my fault, and then I told her that I was moving in with Claire, and that I would be giving up my place. And not a moment too soon, I thought, before they throw me out. It was now well over two months since I'd paid any rent, or since they'd heard a word from me.

"What are you going to do about Paula?" she asked. It was a threatening question that cut straight to the fist-sized pump kachunking in my chest.

"What do you mean?" I answered.

"She can't stay down there, in that neighborhood." The contempt fairly dripped from her voice.

"Why the hell not?" My heart was quickening its pace.

"You've never even been here, you don't know what it's like." In my mind it was an enchanted kingdom of marvelous radicals, free animals like me. Sarah, the conventional one, had an alternate perspective.

"What about school?" she went on. "It would take you over an hour to drive from there to Paula's school, you'd never get her there on time. There's too much driving."

With a grand disregard for tedious, trivial details I said, "I'll just have to get up a little earlier. I can get her there on time." I was sure that my even-tempered tone of resolve would be convincing.

"Alistair," she scoffed, (I'd been meaning to speak to her about her scoff because it was a smoker's scoff), "you can't get her to school on time as it is. Paula told me what happened. And then I got a call from the school, they said that you bring her in late all the time. I just won't go for it. If you want to live with Claire go ahead but it's going to change how you see Paula."

"What the fuck are you talking about?" I screamed into the receiver at the top of my voice. "You don't have any right to tell me that. Where I live is my business," I was fuming, pouring venom into the phone, watch it baby, I'm the Lizard King, don't mess with me, "it has no effect on my rights regarding my daughter."

"Alistair," Sarah said plaintively, "think of it from her point of view. All that time on the road, "it's not safe. And that neighborhood isn't safe either. I can't allow it."

"Allow it," I roared, a Sultan insulted by the effrontery of an uppity peasant. "Who the fuck do you think you're talking to? You're not in any position to allow anything. That's my daughter you're talking about."

Sarah was calm. "We're just going to have to come up with another arrangement. Why can't you keep your place?" Take the high ground, charge the machine-gun nest. I got calm too, calm and evil.

"Look you bitch," I snarled, "I'm going to pick her up tomorrow like I always do and I'm going to bring her back here because this is where I'm living now. Do you understand?"

"I can't let you," Sarah was icy and determined. "It's not the best thing for her." There was a long, horrible silence on the line. "I'm keeping her home tomorrow," she went on, her voice steely with reserve, "I can't let you see her again until we get this thing resolved." She had me straightjacketed, trapped. I blew like the whistle on a steam locomotive.

"You bitch. You cunt. You whore." I shrieked. "I'll nail you to the wall, I'll bury you, how dare you fuck with me you sack of parrot crap." The line went dead leaving me with an imbecilic electronic buzz. It sounded like a swarm of bees circling in my brain. In fury I punched my hand into the plaster wall, pushing right through it. My hand felt like it had been run over by a car. I rushed into the bathroom, smacking the door up against the bureau, which only made me even more furious, and ran it under cold water. I was gasping with pain, I tried squeezing the punished hand between my knees but nothing helped.

"Claire," I yelled, "I need those keys now, I've got to get out of here."

Claire came into the bathroom and looked at the hand. "Are you all right?" she asked, really worried.

"Everything's fine," I bellowed. "I'll be ok, I've just got to go outside and calm down. Goddamn that bitch."

Claire slipped the spare set of keys into my pocket and with heartfelt thanks I kissed her, threw on my jacket and flew down the stairs.

Chapter 30

A Walk On The Wild Side

I burst into the street like an out of control chainsaw. It was late, about one in the morning, dark as doom and as cold as a contract killer's gaze. Very few streetlights out here and the few that do exist have had their bulbs bashed out with rocks, tossed like baseballs, long ago. This is the kind of neighborhood where trash cans get stolen. I had no plan, no destination, just a truckload of rage to burn off. I started striding into the gloom at breakneck speed with a wanton disregard for sidewalk etiquette. Crisscrossing streets, walking in front of moving cars, plowing forward towards Baltimore Avenue, the main drag of the territory.

I stormed into the first joint that was still open, a dive called The Rib Cage. As soon as I stepped inside I saw that I was the only white person in the room. There was a counter in the back where they sold ribs to go but mostly it was a beer and shot spot with a pool table, a jukebox and a cigarette machine. My sense of smell is atrophied from smoking so many cigarettes but I couldn't fail to notice the stench, an unholy blend of charred barbecue sauce, sawdust, stale beer, cigarette smoke and sweat. A far cry from the Four Seasons. Every pair of red-rimmed eyes homed in on me as I stepped up to the bar. The bartender was every bit as impressive as he'd have to be to lord over a pack of ruffians like these, he was bigger than Prince Wilson with a head as clean as Isaac Hayes'. He came over to me slowly, casually, in his own good time.

"What'll it be homeboy?" he said, in a soft-spoken voice rich with authority.

"Shot of bourbon please," the words sprayed out of my mouth like bullets from a machine gun. He set it up and I knocked it back in one gulp, a little fireball roaring through my system. It knocked about two points off my frenzy, I stared straight ahead at my reflection in the mirror behind the bar. I had the wild-eyed look of a terrorist, I frightened my own bad self. I looked around at the sea of black faces, offering a small, non-committal smile, wide enough to telegraph that I meant no harm, not wide enough to lead anyone to believe that I wanted to climb into anyone's head. I'm not here to make trouble. I'm here for comfort.

I remembered an event from a couple of years before when I took my then girlfriend, Barbara, to a blues concert in North Philadelphia. The hall held about five hundred people, the kind of room where they used to hold Bar Mitzvahs until the neighborhood cycled over. At one point I looked at Barbara and very quietly said, "Do you know that we're the only white people in this room?" It was true. Quite an extraordinary experience, I recommend it to every white person in America. Become a minority for a day. Be black for a day, Jewish for a day, queer for a day, poor for a day, it does wonders for your humanity. The most perfect thing about it was that I never felt threatened, I didn't feel hated, on the contrary, I felt welcomed. I was on my best behavior, like everyone else there. I was on a date. I had respect for the music, the occasion, and the people.

Black people are a lot more generous about accepting whites into their ranks than whites are about accepting blacks. When a black person senses that you're human first and white second and think of him as human first and black second, the anger and defensiveness drop off considerably. Did God make people different colors? That was really helpful, thanks pal. Race, I must point out, is a four letter word twice. My sense of unjust degradation burned in me like a holy flame, I faced the world with clenched teeth. I was a white man who despised whites for what they'd done to blacks. An aristocrat who looked down his nose at the wealthy elite for how they exploited the poor in order to feed their vile appetites. A man who condemned males for their cruelty to women. A Christian who boiled with hate at the thought of how Jews had been systematically persecuted and slaughtered. A heterosexual who condemned the pettiness, the small-mindedness, the idiotic queasiness that sired homophobia and helped turn gay into a four letter word which roughly translated means, I think they've slashed my tires. All these groups I was born into carry such a heritage of shame. And of course they compound their sin by trying to rationalize their prejudices, frequently calling on, guess who, Mr. Big Stuff, The Chairman of the Board, God himself, to legitimize their despicable prejudices.

Yes, I was angry. I was sweating, really hot, wiping my forehead. I asked for another bourbon. When the bartender poured out the second shot I raised it carefully to my lips, looked him in the eye and offered up this toast. "Free James Brown." He laughed, then smiled.

"Yeah," he said, ruefully, "they locked up the Godfather. Terrible thing." The bourbon chewed its way through my pipes, how long had it been since I'd eaten?

"How much do I owe you?" I asked, searching my pockets for money.

"That'll be two-fifty, blood," he said, "the second one's on me." I was stunned, stunned and honored. I laid down a five and began to button my jacket. I felt absolutely legitimized, validated, I'd wandered into the belly of the beast and come out with a big old seal of approval. Amazing how far you can go when you don't care anymore.

"Thank you very much," I said, "I'll remember this place." I looked at him admiringly, with a guy like that on my bus I was as safe as the President. In assembling my staff I would surely need a bodyguard, he would do nicely.

"You better put some food in that belly or stop drinking like that," he said, "else your little trolley gonna run off the track." God made priests, Satan made bartenders, sometimes it's too close to call, n'est ce pas?

"I'll see you on the flip side," I said, feeling refreshed and stronger.

"Later, babe," he responded, and went back to wiping the bar. All eyes trained in on my departure, I smiled and waved. McHarg is safe anywhere because McHarg honors the dignity of all souls. I passed through the door, a bloodthirsty mob of one.

I continued my snozzmondilick march down Baltimore Avenue, towards the heart of the city. The bourbon had mellowed me some but it hadn't made me any happier. Where before I was lighter fluid ignited into leaping flames, now I was glowing red coals, less dramatic, more dangerous. I had a lot of heat to walk off and I was going to stick with it as long as it took. No singing now, no whistling, no walking TV set this time, no performance, I was down to the bone. Who the fuck did she think she was, standing between me and my daughter? In days to come, when I was rich and famous, my name on everyone's lips, my lips on everyone's mind, she'd wish she'd been a lot nicer to me when I was down and out. Oh yeah, she'd be all pear halves and caviar then, when I had money to buy enough lawyers to drive her into the stone age, then she'd dance to my tune. Witch, standing between me and my blood.

By now I was by 30th Street Station, gazing across the Schuylkill River. I saw the string of boathouses, outlined in pinpoint white Christmas lights, looking like toy houses, dollhouses, Paula, Goddamnit. I looked at the river curving up and away, a great dark artery carrying black blood into the body of the city. That's it, I'll walk by the river. It's quiet, it's peaceful, room to think, soft ground underfoot instead of this unforgiving pavement. I hooked around past the massive edifice of the Art Museum and climbed down into the beginning of Fairmount Park, the grassy stretches of riverbank. It was desolate, occasionally a car would hiss by like a pissed off serpent but for the most part I was totally alone, walking, trying to wear out my anger. I saw some police barricades, those oversized wooden sawhorses used for directing traffic, long planks held in place by marvelous, oversized A's. Without even thinking about it I picked one up. It was heavy, about six feet long and made of solid wood. I carried it over to the edge of the river and hurled it into the dark water. That felt good. I see a red door and I want it painted black. Thanks Mick Jagged Dagger. Nothing like a little senseless vandalism to help vent a spleen. It felt so good, I threw a few more in. I was surprised by how far I was able to throw them, considering I could barely pick them up. That slug. I'll teach her.

For miles to come, whatever I saw that hit me the wrong way got tossed into the river. Day-glow orange traffic cones flew like giant elves' hats. Hubcaps sailed like pop culture frisbees, General Motors UFOs. Keep Off The Grass signs, here you go fish, something to read. I wish I had more sense of humor sometimes, keepin' the sadness at bay, throwin' some lightness on these things, laughin' it all away. Thanks Joni I think I'll slit my wrists Mitchell. By the time I was five miles up the river I realized what I was doing. I was walking home. Back to Ambler, to my place. I'd already walked ten miles and wasn't even winded. By now I was off the East River Drive and into a residential area. Nice car, think I'll snap off the antenna. Another nice car, let's break off the mirror. Say, that wasn't so hard. A metal For Sale sign, I wonder how far I could throw that? By now I'd been walking for hours, it was getting close to dawn. At last my well of energy began to run dry. My poor hand was throbbing, it was swollen from punching through the wall. My feet were beginning to ache, I was wearing Four Seasons shoes where running shoes would have been appropriate. When I got to the top of Chestnut Hill I finally had to lay down to rest, I was becoming dizzy, I thought I might pass out. I found a grassy spot where I wouldn't be seen and lay down on the hard, frost covered ground. Shivering with cold and face up into the hard, blue sky of morning, I drifted into sleep.

I couldn't have been asleep long when I heard a male voice cry out, "Jesus Christ, are you all right?" A hand was shaking my shoulder. I opened my eyes to see the Sharper Image Catalog concept of a demographic target, a white guy in his early thirties, trimmed out in jogging attire that must have cost more than every cent I had in the world. "Are you all right?" he asked, "do you want me to send for help?" I realized where I was and felt stupid, ashamed, if only I hadn't needed to rest it would have been all right I thought.

"No thanks," I returned, "I'm ok. I just needed to rest for a minute. Thank you though." I got to my feet and began walking again. The remaining miles went more slowly. My feet were beginning to burn, it felt like I was walking on hot nails. But I was almost there, goddamnit, what an incredible effort. My shins were starting to feel tender, my whole body ached. I must have looked like a hobo, horribly out of place among the people cruising by in their Mercedes and BMWs. I wanted to be home very badly, I felt like I'd been thrown into a washing machine. When at last I did get to my house I collapsed on the floor. Twenty-six miles I'd walked, almost without a stop. Leaving a trail of debris behind me. But it had worked. I wasn't angry anymore. I was too tired to feel angry, too spent. All I wanted was a warm bath to relax my muscles and a quiet place to sleep. If I could have crawled into the dark comfort of a womb I would have done it in an instant.

Chapter 31

You Take The High Road, And I'll Take The Low Road

Mania and Depression are two sides of the same coin. They don't *look* the same, but they function in the same way. And they end up in the same place.

I went without a major Manic episode from 1970 to 1986, the year I got divorced. The price I paid for this serenity was a Depression that became a way of life. My mother died. My father got remarried and quickly began a second family, a second family which had no room for reminders of the first family. The old, golden life was gone, replaced by emptiness. My brother was away in med school, I hardly ever saw him. Every other relative I had in the world lived in Europe. I was cut off in a way that was completely new to me.

In my heart I was certain that I couldn't make it on my own. I was driven into marriage more by terror than by moonlight.

Sarah was and is both smart and competent. She was the boss, consistently reinforcing every negative thought I had about myself. My Depression was not of the weeping and hand wringing variety, it was of the "Kick Me" sign on the butt variety. I lost touch with my old life altogether, letting my friendships atrophy. So I became the creation of her world alone, a world in which she made all of the major decisions. I don't fault her for it. All of us are what we are and we pick who we pick for very complicated reasons. But it was an unhealthy, perverse paradigm. It didn't *look* as sick and demented as Mania, but it was.

Of course, in seven years, one is likely to stumble over a little happiness, just as in the Mania there are moments of clarity. Restoring the house together. The clubbing in New Hope, when we were like two kids playing in a sandbox. The years when my one-man advertising agency was working out, before bad-pay clients drove me to ruin, confirming every dreadful suspicion she had about my ability to be a provider. The bicycle vacation through Vermont, the prelude to Paula's birth. When we got divorced, the people we knew were stunned. It looked like a picture-perfect life.

But sometimes the old masters painted over paintings, sometimes more than once, because canvases and frames were scarce and expensive. In the process of restoring a lovely seventeenth century landscape, the museum employee discovers that there's an entirely different painting underneath. Something scented with the breath of Hieronymous Bosch.

In the Depression of those years I painted myself into a rarified, highly-specific world, inaccessible to other people. I shored-up a wildly unrealistic view of myself by seeking out a situation where my faults were constantly celebrated and anything which might feed my strengths was denied. I fled the challenge of grappling with the realities of life by turning over that odious task to another person.

I focused on the veneer, the illusion, and fled the reality. I had lots of time to talk about what color to paint our lovely Bucks County house but no time to talk about the lack of love, dignity, and kindness in it.

I undermined myself. If I'd given my business one hundred percent, I could have made it a hit. I was my own worst enemy, subconsciously sabotaging myself, reconfirming the lie of Depression, reconfirming my dark self-image. Preventing myself from winning.

Mania and Depression are twin assassins sent by the same General. One kills you by mixing in a little sprinkling of ground glass with every meal you consume, until your insides are shredded and bleeding. The other attaches electrical wires to your most sensitive spots and turns on the voltage until you twitch like an epileptic and the air fills with the smell of smoke. Two ways of getting the job done. Two ways that work equally well.

Remembering that horrible phone call with Sarah and the marathon, furious walk which followed brought all of this home for me. I saw how the shiny surface of my Manic euphoria cracked, revealing the tempest within. Aching sorrow mixed with rage, self-punishment, panic, and desperate energy. Sarah had jabbed an icepick into my Achilles' heel.

As Stevie Wonder said, with an emotional purity which always makes me cry the same way Dr. King's "I Have A Dream" speech makes me cry, "Everybody's Got A Weakness In Life, Girl You Just Happen To Be Mine." Of course, Paula is my weakness. Let the fates do their worst to me, let them rain fire, I don't really care and I've seen it before. I can stand it, as long as they leave *her* alone.

I'd gladly give up my life to save that little girl, and it's wonderful to feel that way about anybody or anything.

I was almost unreachable in my Mania. Without intending to, Sarah had found the one way to contact the real me. My response, raining war like a Norse god, showed that the real me did *not* want to be contacted by the real world. But it was too late. Contact had been made.

Confronting a person in the throes of full Mania is a really risky proposition. Manic grandeur and enormous optimism can turn to savage denial in seconds. The level of intensity stays constant. Good nature becomes passionate anger, high-handed impatience, rage. I know that in those moments my Mania, that is, my Manic self, possessed the same, unqualified dedication to self-preservation seen in cornered animals. Although I'm a committed Pacifist by training and by inclination, this conscious philosophy meant nothing at the time. With my physical size and strength, the added strength of adrenaline, my desperate rage, and my red hot anger with the world which was beginning to close in on me, I'm certain that I could easily have beaten a man's face into hamburger.

And enjoyed every minute of it.

Just a word to the wise. Don't spit into the wind, don't step on Superman's cape, and don't fuck around with a guy who's Manic.

As I raced those endless miles, destroying everything in my path, I roared like a wounded bear. I screamed, I raved, I wailed. I had the Manic energy, but my soul was filled with the despair of Depression. Real Depression, the Depression of a man who no longer wants to live. Mania and Depression swirled and blew together in me, a maelstrom, like black and white clouds on a March day. It was all one thing. My entire being was just one raw nerve. All I could feel was pain.

Every trip up and every trip down takes a little more out of me, every trip away from the real thing.

When I'm Manic, I say that although the glass is now only half full of water, soon there will be a thousand glasses, and they will all be full of champagne. When I'm Depressed, I say the glass is half empty, and all tap water today is dangerously polluted anyway, and Lord isn't it tragic how many of the world's citizens are dying of thirst? In either case I'm wrong, it's just the projection of my wildly variable moods onto reality. It's always the same glass.

When I'm well, when I'm healthy, when I'm me, is when I'm capable of saying, the glass is currently at fifty percent capacity, and at the moment it contains water.

And water is life.

Chapter 32

Shattered Glass

That evening we spoke at length about the particulars of our relationship. We agreed that the back room would be mine, for me to use however I wished. Claire would not enter it unless asked, this was her idea. Since she ran her home as an unofficial rooming house she liked to be very clear about house rules and issues of privacy. In exchange I would contribute money when I found work. Likewise, I would contribute money for food when I found work. In the meantime, I could earn my keep by working on the house. This arrangement suited me fine since I couldn't wait to transform the place. In my mind I'd already gotten rid of almost all of Claire's flea market rubbish and painted the place, using the Four Seasons as my model. We were officially trying the living together experiment.

The next morning, feeling much more secure than I had in days, I called Sarah to make amends. This turned out to be a lot harder than I'd expected. Sarah told me that I'd forced her to do something she really didn't want to do. She'd gotten a restraining order, prohibiting me from seeing Paula. My comments on the phone had convinced her that I was a threat to the safety of them both. She'd notified the school. Until she was convinced that I was compos mentis again she said there would be no contact between me and my daughter. Her deadly serious delivery told me there was no talking her out of it, not now. I felt like I'd been blindsided by a tank.

This was the first problem I'd encountered in months that I wasn't able to solve in half a second. I told her I'd get back to her after I'd had a chance to think about what I could do to satisfy her that things were all right. Temporarily stunned into numb immobility, I quickly bounded back. I told Claire I was going to do another run to get some more of my stuff and within minutes I was back on the road. After packing my car to the gills I drove over to the Newport House for a snort. I was reeling, I needed a treat. In my car were many of the things most important to me, including both sets of car keys. I parked the black sedan in the lot, carefully checking the contents with a visual scan. I didn't want anything of obvious value to be visible. I was way out on a limb, these were some of my most prized possessions, exposed for the world to see. Satisfied at last that I could safely leave the car I jumped out, pushed down the lock, thus locking all the doors, and slammed the door shut. The moment after I'd done it I knew I was in trouble. There, in plain sight, lying on the dashboard, were both sets of keys. I burned with rage. Hadn't I suffered enough? No chance of calling a locksmith, I didn't have the patience to wait or the money to pay. I certainly wasn't going to go into the restaurant and ask for a coat hanger to break into a car loaded with stuff. Too suspicious. I was fucked, pure and simple. I needed a solution fast and I needed it to be on my terms.

The answer was obvious. I found a large rock and smashed out an opera window on my dear car, the famous Invisible Driving car. It hurt, it was like cutting myself with a knife. But it had to be done. McHarg breaks into his own car. No thought of doing a set now, my confidence was blown. It would take money to fix that window, money I didn't have, and without it fixed the car was begging to be stolen. And in Claire's neighborhood, a car didn't have to ask twice. In fact, if a car merely hinted that it might enjoy being stolen, it had a date. Mr. Suave Sophisticate was screwing up, losing his touch, it rattled me. I drove to Claire's cautiously, blushing beneath an enormous invisible dunce cap.

As I carried my precious possessions through the living room and up the stairs I overheard Ultraviolet and Prince

Wilson talking. As usual, they ignored me. At one point I heard Ultraviolet say, "I have to go to Pittsburgh but I can't decide if I want to take an airplane or just astral-project." I laughed to myself. These two just had to go. Being Bohemian was one thing, being out of your fucking mind was another. The back room was beginning to look like a garage but I was still hopeful. With time and work I would take over the entire house and then I could safely spread my things throughout. This was just a temporary measure. I would transform the place. Sarah would see that it was all right. Paula would be staying overnight here in no time. This was just a rough stretch of road.

That evening Claire and I talked for hours. It was comforting. In Claire's mind, every problem has a solution if one is willing to be innovative. Claire the Queen of workshops, the absolute liberal. In Claire's circle of friends if you weren't at least bi-sexual you were considered square. She had even spent time in a lesbian relationship herself although she'd decided in the end that it wasn't for her. Still, she had many homosexual friends, both male and female. And the workshops. Masturbation workshops. Channeling. Changing the world of form through positive meditation. Learning how to heal the inner child. Group dynamics. Massage therapy. Past life workshops. Witchcraft training. Claire's approach to philosophical issues makes Shirley MacLaine look like a pedantic Oxford classics professor. There's a fuzzy sloppiness to her thinking that I find laughable but still, it has a soothing quality. Mainly because it allows for all possibilities. No rules, no absolutes. Claire believes that ultimately at the center of everything is mystery. That when you touch mystery, you touch the very heart of life itself.

"You're hurting right now," she said, "because you can't see your daughter. But you'll fix that. In the meantime, you know she's all right. You just have to be a little bit patient." We were lying in bed. I was so grateful to be with her, grateful for her steadiness. While she may subscribe to some pretty bizarre ideas, there's something centered about Claire. It was getting late, she dozed off to sleep. I couldn't sleep. I had to get busy or I would think about Paula too much. I went out to walk.

On Baltimore Avenue I found a diner that was still open. I went in to get cigarettes and a coffee to go, walking companions. The black woman behind the counter looked me up and down, got the cigarettes, and then got the coffee.

"You want any cream and sugar in that, darlin'?" she asked.

I looked at her, my good humor returning. "No thanks, I want it black. Extra black."

She let out a good natured giggle. "Well I brewed it myself," she laughed, "that black enough for you?"

You're so good, bless you, I need people with me, people on my bus. "Now I guess you want me to pay," I went on. "I'll be paying for this in cash, do I get a cash discount?"

She laughed at me again.

"No good, huh, well how about a funny white guy discount?"

She whooped, putting my change on the counter. I beamed with appreciation, liking her for liking me. I still had it, I was going to be fine. Just bumps on the road. Out the door he goes, into the bitter chill of a February night, walking a little more slowly on tenderized feet.

I was heading into town, brooding, unsettled. The anger was returning. I was whistling in time to the footsteps, elevating my mood. By the time I got to City Hall I was back up to full steam. The streets were close to empty, the occasional hooker, bum, street urchin. I was standing next to the City Hall tower, looking straight up, being observed by a wretched, homeless waif wound up in rags, sitting on one of the benches. Pigeons were all around me, City Hall seems to be the capitol of pigeon activity in the city, and the fountainhead of pigeon shit. They were walking all around me, annoyingly close to my feet. Dirty, grimy, urban pigeons, completely accustomed to dodging people as they compete for bits of pretzels and whatever other garbage collects on the streets. What revolting birds, what a poor job of representing their species they do. Complete disregard for sidewalk etiquette, always getting in the way. Filthy pieces of shit.

I shot my foot down to crush one, missed it, and ended up tramping down hard on a big pile of dog shit instead. I walked towards the Four Seasons to use their bathroom to clean up the mess. When I got there and had a chance to see my shoes in the light I realized what a disgusting mess they actually were, at least one of them. Then I had a thought. People leave their shoes out at hotels overnight to be shined. I hopped an elevator and got off at the second floor. Sure enough, there was a nice pair of shoes sitting outside one of the rooms. Faster than you could say 'strippers wear slippers' I eased out of my shoes and into the others. They were just a bit too big, but, all things considered, fit pretty nicely. I felt badly about soiling my own nest, so to speak, pulling this rotten move in the Four Seasons, but times were tough and I wasn't about to work my magic wearing shoes covered with dog crap. There are many ways to upgrade a wardrobe, and some of them are legal. God knows what the maid thought when she came to collect the shoes, and what the guest thought when he got them back.

Chapter 33

If You Can't Trust Yourself, Then Who Can You Trust?

For me, the crash is the most dangerous and horrifying part of a Manic episode. During the crash I stare into the bloodshot eyes of a really hideous truth. I cannot truly trust myself.

I'm potentially a threat to my own safety. I'm potentially a threat to other people, even to the people I love.

My good-old reliable brain, the brain that kept me dancing through college, grad school, marriage, in fact, dancing through life in general without ever even working that hard, is not as faithful as I believed.

When I crash I go from Fred Astaire, dancing smoothly on a marble floor, to Alistair, dancing spasmodically on a carpet of splintered glass. In bare feet. Keeping that broad, false smile on my face grows harder and harder, until it becomes impossible.

Then, at last, so many tears. Not crocodile tears. Real tears.

As an insecure egotist, an individualist, I always, always relied on my mind to amuse me, sustain me, protect me. It did. It was more reliable than any church, any government, any friend. It got me out of one scrape after another, including those times when another person got dangerously close to really touching me. But the crash is where I discover that far from saving me from a catastrophe, my mind is guilty of creating one.

I feel shame and self-hatred. I feel sold out and betrayed by my oldest, wisest, and most stalwart friend. I'm terrified.

My mind has made a fool of me, a public spectacle whose dreadful stupidity is out on the street for everyone to ridicule and despise. Instead of looking down on others from my solitary height, now it's me who's low, the object of scorn. I'm the worst kind of fool there is, a fool who isn't funny. Suddenly nothing makes sense. I have to reinvent myself. I have to start from scratch.

As I plunge headfirst into the wreckage that survives my Maniacal sprees of unhinged optimism, the evidence is staggering and embarrassing. As ugly as a warthog. As incontrovertible as a smoking gun with my fingerprints. If I'm man enough to deal with my shit, and I have to be, to be worth anything at all, then I'm forced to face it with merciless honesty. Study it with a cold eye. Think long and hard about what's happened, and how it got that way. (Assuming I can even remember what the hell happened. There are large blank spots when I try to remember my episodes.) I'm forced to admit that the chaos around me is *my* chaos, the product of my demented craft.

I must sincerely admit it, and then, with all due contrition and sorrow, get over it. Go on. So easy to say, so very nearly impossible to do.

After that comes the boring part. Nothing more complex than old-fashioned work. Get out the mop, get out the broom, and clean up the whole goddamn mess.

The danger of crashing into a backbreaking Depression is enormous. The ordeal of redemption takes place in its own bitter, friendless, horrifying time. It's the loneliest and most painful time my heart has ever known. I often marvel that I survived it, indeed, survived it more than once. Ultimately, the wreckage must be faced by me and me alone, only I can solve the problems I've created. And they're mean. Mean and cold-blooded.

As the inevitability of the crash draws closer, my denial gets increasingly desperate. The flair and panache go raggedy, like the tattered edges of a flag too long at sea, whipped by too many storms. My confidence gets shaken, my behavior becomes more and more reckless, more blatantly out of control. Reality wants to talk to me but I'm not ready. In all three Manic episodes, when I was at this point, I was a lightning rod for trouble.

There's a whole lot of yardage between thinking I'm a Greek god and thinking I'm a destitute, unemployed, whacked-out looney-toon. That's no overnight trip. And because I'm never in a mood to take that trip, the evidence of my plight has to pile high before I'm even willing to consider that I'm unsafe, unwell, and desperately unhappy.

Eventually it piles up so high that I'm trapped by it.

Chapter 34

Outdoor Life

Key. Such a funny little word. A tiny piece of metal that carries a lot of weight. My keychains are getting more and more stylized. I alter them all the time, something to do with my fidgeting energy. They have bonus points, wire snakes, penknives, winding colored cord, they're beginning to look like ceremonial artifacts in an anthropological museum. But as I approached the door of my townhouse, to gather another load of belongings to take to Claire's, I was unable to slip the house key into the door. I checked to make sure I wasn't trying to use one of the keys to Claire's house. I wasn't. Then I looked carefully at the lock. It was new. The motherfuckers had changed the locks on my house, with half of my stuff still in there. I checked the window, it was as tight as a leech in an armpit.

Starting to sweat with panic I raced around to the back of the house to see if I could pry open the sliding glass door. No chance. There was a wooden pole resting in the track, making it impossible to budge. I thought of breaking a window but decided against it. Too risky. And besides, it would leave the place vulnerable to anybody who came after me. I went back to the front of the house and peered in the window. The living room look abused, my stuff was strewn all over the floor in an incoherent jambalaya. And my landlord had seen it like that, shit. Well there's no sense in crying over innocent men who couldn't afford good lawyers and fried in the electric chair, as the old saying goes. Speaking of which, do you know how to tell the difference between a lawyer and a prostitute? Neither do I. Well, I thought, at least I got my important things out. Time to cut and run. A clean break from the past. I was installed at Claire's, that was the main thing. I'd call my landlord and explain the situation, we'd work it out. I owed him a lot of money by now, thousands, and my dollars were dwindling down to a precious few. Obviously I couldn't afford to pay him, I'd have to shmooze him. Christ, my To Do list was becoming as long as a line at a Russian grocery store. Straighten things out with Sarah and Paula. Get my soon to be ex-landlord to let me retrieve the rest of my worldly goods. Free James Brown. Restore Claire's house so it looked like a photo spread in Architectural Digest instead of the tomb of the unregistered voter. Start to talk to my contacts in my spots about singing, to get my career in gear. Teach white people and black people to live in harmony. Talk the homeless back into the mainstream. Pay off the mountain of bills I'd incurred. And these were just the most obvious ones.

I drove back to Claire's, there was nothing else to do. It was a cold, clear evening but I was so angry I didn't even feel like doing any Invisible Driving. Unlike the real universe, my universe seemed to be shrinking. I hadn't seen Paula in days, it gnawed at me. I felt guilty about it and victimized all at once. I'd been severed from my old place, not when I was ready to do it, but by an outside force. Control had been wrestled out of my restless hands. My freedom of movement was severely limited by my lack of funds, in recent days I'd taken to ordering water at the Four Seasons to save myself the price of the drink. Water was free. Then I'd tease the bartenders by asking them to compute twenty seven percent of zero so that I could leave an appropriate tip. The laughs, and my abdomen, are getting thinner. When I got back to Claire's I said hello quickly, told her what had happened, and sealed myself in my room. I took her at her word. It was my room now, she would not come in unless asked. I wanted to stew, I wanted to be alone, I wanted to twirl like a whirling dervish and transform my anger into activity.

I put on one of my tapes, the hottest one I could find, high-pitch funky energy that sizzled with snazzjungulation. I danced around the room to the music, waving my arms like wings, Satan's eager apprentice. I dipped into the vodka and pot, both were running low. Add that to my list of things to do. Fuck it, he said, in rhythm, in sync, slithering in the beat, that's another problem, he said, in rhythm, for another day. I was living in the beat, talking in time, dancing. But it was like dancing in a phone booth. Christ, I thought, the size of my world has shrunk to this, this room, that's my entire domain. And look at it, it's a fucking garage sale waiting to happen. My stuff is good, it's all crammed together, but at least it's good stuff. But look at Claire's shit. It's junk. I'm the guy who can work alchemy and change trash into art but this stuff is beyond even my prodigious abilities. It's low-grade trash and it's clogging up my room.

Well, that was the limit. I'd suffered enough indignity for a day. I opened the windows and welcomed in the biting, winter air. The rocking chair, the one with the hideous pattern, was the first thing to go. It landed with a splat in the backyard of a neighbor and crashed into pieces. Ah yes. Sweet release. A blow against the empire of crumminess, make space for the excellence of the new order. The dogs were barking. I barked back, egging them on. Next came the bookshelves, shoddy, crummy, hollow shelves of the thinnest plywood artlessly constructed to resemble solid wood and covered with a peeling plastic laminate paper which was stamped with a wood pattern in a color unknown to any tree found in nature. I sent them sailing off into the ruins next door, they clattered as they slapped against the bricks. I need room, I need space, how can I create a masterpiece when I'm surrounded by this shit? I heard Claire banging on the door.

"I need to know what you're doing in there," she was yelling.

"Go away," I screamed back, "I can't talk about it right now." I had my eye on a plastic lamp I'd detested since the moment I'd first laid eyes on it. It resembled an abstracted mushroom, constructed of parts so cheap and flimsy that the weight of the cord alone could pull it across the desk. To make it worse, as if that were possible, it was broken and had been amateurishly repaired so that the top rested askew, a mushroom tipping its hat. As I flung it out the window it flew into pieces before it was anywhere near the ground.

"Let me in," Claire was yelling. I'd jammed the doors shut with chairs under the doorknobs. She tried both doors, but couldn't budge either of them. I knew she'd thank me later, someone had to break the logjam. Someone had to show her that only the best was good enough. Someone had to take responsibility for driving mediocrity out of the realm, banishing it to the hinterlands. I stopped to take a breath, my eyes darting around the room, trying to decide on the next piece to purge. Then I heard a crash at the door, the metal dining room chair that had been holding it closed collapsed, the legs giving way like the legs of a drunk about to fall down a flight of stairs.

Prince Wilson stood before me, his enormous body filling up the entire doorframe. "Get out," he said. "Get out now and you won't get hurt." I went cold in an instant. An ex-con, built like a truck, no friend of mine, he could disassemble me without even putting forward his best effort. I was trapped, and I was scared for my life. Even in my fiercest, strongest incarnation I was no match for this guy. "She wants her keys back," he added in his deep, threatening voice. Fumbling, shaking, panicking, I got Claire's keys off my keychain and put them on the desk, I didn't even want to touch him to put them in his hand. I grabbed my coat, stuffed a few basic articles in my pockets, and walked down the hall. He followed me closely down the steps. Claire was in the living room. She looked at me sadly.

"Don't worry about your things," she said, "I won't touch anything. But you've got to get out. You can call me and we'll figure out what to do." I didn't have a thing to say. I just wanted to escape the situation with all of my arms and legs intact. Prince Wilson let me out the door, I heard it being locked behind me. I got into my car quickly and started it up to get the heat going.

It was frighteningly cold outside, I craved the comfort of that heat. I looked around my car, my mini-limo. I realized that my universe had shrunk even further. I stuffed a pillow in the hole where the opera window used to be, I couldn't afford to lose the warmth. With absolutely no idea of where I was going I put the car in gear, released the handbrake, and crept down the street into the unforgiving blackness.

Chapter 35

Tour Cancelled

I didn't have a home, but at least I was free to move. My car was like a second home anyway, and besides, I'd patch things up with Claire soon and everything would be fine again. But where to go now? It was the middle of the night, nothing was open. Even my spots would be deserted at this time of night. I drove aimlessly, there was no harbor for me, no chink in the wall to nestle into. Without thinking about it I found myself driving back to Ambler, towards my townhouse. I didn't want to keep driving indefinitely, it was a waste of gas and gas cost money and I was out of money. But instead of driving to my townhouse I drove into the parking lot of my old employer, Honeywell. The building had a huge parking lot and I reasoned that it would be a quiet, deserted place to stay. I wouldn't be bothering anybody. I turned off the engine and wondered what to do. There was a lot of time left until dawn, until it made sense to call Claire. My car looked like a rat's nest, there was rubbish all over the floor, spillage from the many moving trips. Well, I thought, here's a good opportunity to clean it out. And just for good measure, I'll leave the trash in Honeywell's parking lot. Just a little souvenir to let them know how I feel about them.

I began to dump trash on the asphalt. I may not have much, I thought, but at least I'm caring for what I do have. I had all four doors open, even the trunk was open. Then I saw car lights cruising towards me from the opposite end of the lot. Having survived a personal threat from Prince Wilson and lived to tell about it the last thing I wanted was another encounter where I felt in danger. Was it punks looking for trouble? I had no idea. Quickly I closed the trunk, closed the back doors, jumped in and closed the front doors. I started the engine. By now the car was close by, it pulled up behind me diagonally, leaving me no room to pull out. I saw that it was a police car. What the fuck is this, I thought, I'm on private property, I haven't done anything wrong. And this was no security guard, this was an honest to Satan cop car.

I saw an officer get out and walk over towards me, he had more shit hanging off his belt than a carpenter. I started to panic. He shined a flashlight on me and gestured for me to roll down my window. I opened it a couple of inches. He leaned over and spoke into the crack. Looking around the car as he spoke he said, "Could I see your driver's license and registration, please?" For days I hadn't had any idea where they were, misplaced in the course of the endless shuffling I was always engaged in. The insurance on the car had lapsed, my registration had lapsed, it had been quite a while since the car had been legal.

"Fuck you," I said, "I don't have to show you anything." The officer was big, in his mid-forties, and wearing the humorless expression of a White House security agent. He called something out and his partner emerged from the car and came over and joined him.

"Step out of the car," he said, moving back slightly to allow me room to open the door. To leave my car would have meant leaving the only security I had left, the only remaining armor, there was no way in God's green earth I was going to get out.

"I haven't done anything wrong," I yelled, "I'm sitting in a parking lot. What do you want from me?" The officer reached in and grabbed my hair, pulling it hard, yanking my head over to the window. Somehow he squeezed his other arm through the window and pulled up the lock. His partner tugged open the door, pulling the officer's hand and my head along with it. I pushed the butt of my hand into the bridge of the younger cop's nose and he dropped like a marionette. But the first cop got around behind me and tangled me up in a chokehold. I was terrified, I thought these fuckin' storm troopers wanted to kill me. The big cop dragged me down to the ground, we rolled over and over, trading frantic blows, grunting, grabbing. I was squirming like an alligator trying to slip out of his grasp but he was just too good for me. I felt the gravel scratching my face and his entire weight on my back. He squashed my neck to the ground with a nightstick, choking me, defeating me. Then the younger one came over and put on handcuffs, hands behind my back.

"You little turd," he said, when they'd gotten me immobilized, and gave me a swift, sincere kick in the stomach. I curled up in pain, out of breath, totally terrified. Whump, another kick, big black boot. I gasped, I couldn't breathe in. Then one more, almost where it hurts the most, I screamed through clenched teeth.

"Don't leave marks, asshole," the big one said. I fought to get my breath back. What if these guys weren't cops? What if they were psychopaths who liked to dress up like cops and kill people?

"*Help*," I started screaming when I could breathe again, "these crazy motherfuckers are trying to kill me." I was crying with fear. Humiliated, powerless, shivering with terror, wondering if I was about to die. "Somebody help me, somebody call the police." The cops were now a bit more composed, they'd seemed frightened at first.

"Get him into the car fast," said the big one to the young one. The young one, who wore a nasty, vindictive leer which said to me I'm too fuckin' stupid to get any other work and I really enjoy having power over people who are superior to me and you hurt my nose asshole and I'm enjoying this so much I'd gladly do it for free took me to the police car and stuffed me into the back seat the way a person stuffs an empty cereal box into an overfull trash can, making sure that I smacked my forehead on the roof of the car in the process. I was horrified by both of them but the idea that the young one could legally use a gun drove me into despair. He was the kind of person who under slightly different circumstances would have become a cheap hoodlum. The kind of punk who delights in making peoples' lives miserable.

So now I was sitting in the back seat, looking at the miniature cyclone fence which separated the world of those who sit in the front seat and have guns and talk on radios and write out citations from the world of the back seat which is populated by niggers, junkies, homeless wretches, and honorary niggers for a day like me. I sat in the back shaking with fear, crying, wondering how the fuck I was going to get out of this. Both of the cops got into the car and closed the doors.

"What's your business here?" The big one.

"I used to work here. I was driving. I was tired. I just needed a rest."

"So why is there crap all over the place?"

"I was cleaning out my car."

"Why?"

"Why not? Is there a law against cleaning out your car that I don't know about?"

"No but there is a law against punching a police officer in the face," the young one spat back. He was so smug because he had me and there was nothing I could do about it. I was starting to understand. It would be my word against theirs and they were cops and I was an out of work guy with no money.

"But you provoked it," I screamed. "I hit you in self-defense. This thug pulled me out of the car just because I refused to show my license." Why was I trying to use reason with these guys? "You beat up on me and I try to defend myself and all of a sudden there's a crime, I don't get it. The only victim of a crime around here is me."

"I'm going to have to take you in," the big one said calmly.

I saw my freedom slipping away like sand through an hourglass and I didn't even begin to have the ammunition to do anything about it. Me, the guy who can't voluntarily sit still for ten minutes, caged. I was sweating like a guilty con lying on the witness stand.

"What for?" I shrieked.

"Drunk driving, creating a disturbance, resisting arrest, assaulting an officer."

"Drunk driving," I hollered, incredulous. "I was sitting in a parking lot for Chrissake."

"We'll talk about it at the station," the big one went on. He pulled away, leaving my little car, my home for the moment, alone in the vast parking lot. My mood began to change. The cuffs held my wrists behind me, but I still had my mind, and my mouth.

"You know," I said to both of them, "you're making a big mistake." I was calmer now. "I know a lot of lawyers. This is a bad bust. You don't have anything on me. You might want to drop this now. I can always file a suit against you for wrongful arrest and brutality." No response at all. I waited a few moments and then asked, "Would you tell me something?"

"What?" said the young one, impatient and gruff.

"How long does it take you guys to inflate your shoes?"

"What?" said the young one again, genuinely confused.

"If I squeezed your nose, would it honk?"

"I'll squeeze *your* nose, you shit," said the young one, turning back to face me.

"Leave him alone," said the big one. "He thinks he's funny. We'll give him a little time to think about how funny he is. Let him try his jokes out on the Captain."

"Your Captain's last name isn't Barnum by any chance is it?" They didn't respond. Sweating, unable to sit comfortably with my wrists cuffed together behind me, I watched the night landscape. Barren terrain, closed shops staring back at me with black eyes. Well lit, empty parking lots. No signs of life. Where before the suburbs had seemed benign, secure, and pastoral, if dull, now the stillness filled me with haunting dread. No room for the one who does not fit in these well-tended shruburbs. I was different, no trying to deny it. But I'd always thought that being different was wonderful. Now I realized that here being different meant that you were pulled up by your roots like an offending dandelion.

We arrived at the station and I was ushered in unceremoniously, an officer on each arm. In Claire's neighborhood children were being killed in the crossfire as rival drug lords dispensed frontier justice in drive-by, gangland-style executions, turf wars. There's real crime, I thought, the Philadelphia police could sure use a hand with that. But these morons have nothing better to do than pick me up for littering in a parking lot. You might have thought I was Al Capone from the attention I was getting. They took me downstairs into a small room with no windows. It was cinderblock, brightly lit, and painted in a combination of cream and industrial strength olive green, a color I've always associated with bureaucratic architecture. All the warmth of an abattoir. They sat me down in a plain, wooden chair, hands still cuffed behind me.

"Could you take these cuffs off?" I asked, thinking it a very reasonable request, "I'm obviously not going to escape." I was squirming like a worm on the end of hook, writhing nonstop with anxiety.

"Shut up," said the young one. "Sit still."

The Captain came into the room. You could almost hear the average IQ level drop. He looked incredibly young, tall, sandy hair. He'd probably been the center on his high school basketball team, athletic, competitive. As white as mayonnaise on Wonderbread. All three of them were white, big surprise there, so white they made me feel black. They were young, white and thick as posts. I looked at these three dime-store thugs, pipsqueaks who wouldn't last a night in North Philadelphia, and realized full force that my fate was in the hands of people who were younger than me, less intelligent than me, nastier than me, less worldly-wise than me, and it made me as agitated as a cockroach surprised in the middle of the kitchen floor when you've switched on the light past midnight. I didn't know which way to go first.

The Captain listened to the older arresting officer tell his story and told them to give me a breath test to see if I was drunk. I wasn't drunk. But all they could think of was that I was drunk. Maybe if police officers were more broad minded, etc. etc. etc. Maybe if politicians were honest, yabba dabba doo. Maybe if I had some ham, and a roll, I could make a ham and cheese sandwich, if I had some cheese. So the three of them brought out the breath test machine.

"I'm not drunk," I insisted, pleading with them. As I watched these three cops wrestle with this machine the only thing that came to mind as I marveled at their utter ineptitude was the Three Stooges. If this was happening to somebody else, I thought, it would be incredibly funny. But I had to wait, patiently, while these twits agonized over the fine points of getting this machine to work. Three apes contemplating an artifact from an alien civilization. At last they gave up. Great, I thought, there goes the drunk driving bust, they can't even get their own stupid machine to work. The arresting officer began to question me about my license, about the car. I gave him the information and he entered it into a computer terminal to verify it. We all waited for the response. Four men who fate had determined might enjoy sitting together for a while in the basement of a police station in the middle of the night. He looked positively hurt when the information came back showing that I was who I said I was, that I had a valid license, and that I did own the car. Thank God, I thought, that it didn't point out that the insurance on the car had lapsed and that the registration had too.

"Get up," barked the arresting officer. The fact that these guys had nothing on me didn't seem to discourage them at all. They showed no signs of letting me go. Not knowing what to expect, I stood up.

"The Captain thinks you're on drugs," the arresting officer said. "We're going to take off the cuffs for a minute so you can take your clothes off. We're going to search you and your clothes."

I just cried. I was terrified. Humiliated, degraded, powerless, outnumbered, shaking with misery, sobbing. The two officers gripped my wrists as the Captain unlocked the cuffs. Quickly they took off my jacket and shirt and as soon as they had, to my horrified disbelief, they put the cuffs back on. Sitting me back in the chair they took off my pants, shoes, and socks. I was choking with fear, feeling incredibly vulnerable. These large men with their uniforms, badges, guns, radios, nightsticks, handcuffs, decked out like soldiers, warriors, me, sitting in a chair, hands again cuffed behind me, in only my underpants. That was the only dignity they left me, those vicious motherfuckers, at least they didn't strip me naked. Mercifully my toenails were no longer painted, I couldn't even begin to imagine how much fun they would have had with that.

They started to search my pockets. Soon the desk was covered with lighters, books of matches from the Four Seasons and all the other swank spots in town worth knowing about, bonus points, my little wire snakes, (don't fail me now my little reptiles, I thought, bite them), a very small amount of change, a wallet, keys, three different packs of cigarettes, all different brands, (thank God I'd put the pot in the glove compartment), assorted phrases ripped from brochures to be used in collages at a later date, the phrase "Face It" lay prominently on the desk, a spare pair of socks I happened to be carrying, a reptile tape, an envelope full of my favorite photographs, the mouthpiece for a soprano saxophone, some poems on horribly crumpled paper, and a wire heart I had made for Paula, intending to drop it in Sarah's mailbox with a note.

"Jesus Christ," said the younger of the thugs who'd arrested me, "look at this shit." I was heartsick, it may have looked like trash but it was *my* trash, strewn about for these rednecks to contemplate. I felt violated, secretless. A freak on display for the amusement of imbeciles. Well, I reasoned, it's a fucking mess but there's nothing incriminating in there. Being weird isn't a crime yet, or have they changed the laws?

"Maybe he stashed it in the coal chute," said the younger one, as cold as a contract killer's nastier younger brother. When I realized what he meant I felt as though my soul was straining to escape from my body, I felt a cold sweat coming on. Loudly this defender of the public peace snapped on a rubber glove, the smacking sound hurt as much as a slap on the face would have. I jumped. He yanked me to a standing position, pulled my underpants down, and jammed what felt like fourteen unlubricated fingers up my rectum. I screamed in pain.

"You motherfucker," I bellowed. "You motherfucker. Do the smart thing and kill me because if you don't I'm gonna eat your badge and shit it out as tinsel." I felt like I was passing a pineapple. "You're dogmeat trailer trash, you're gatorbait. I'm gonna cut your dick off with a rusty razor blade." He relented, having found only what belonged, and I collapsed on the chair. I closed my eyes and sobbed uncontrollably, biting my lip, trying to stop.

Once again they undid the cuffs and one on each arm led me to a cell. I didn't have any resistance left in me, I was still crying. They pushed me into the tiny cell, threw in my clothes after me, and slammed the door. Like a child who's just witnessed the dismemberment of his favorite stuffed animal, I sat crying, slowly putting my clothes back on. When I was done I realized that they hadn't included my belt. Do these morons think I'm going to hang myself, I wondered. I managed to regain some composure. I began to make deals with God, just in case there actually was one. Get me out of this, I thought, and I'll never eat pork again. Hell, you make the deal, I never knew what you wanted from me anyway. Name it, I'll do it. But don't let these miserable bastards kill me, they're insane. They're vicious. They're so excited to have a real, live criminal on their hands they don't know how to contain themselves. I guess they really take littering seriously out here in the suburbs. The door opened.

Cuffs back on, I was once again in the backseat of the squad car. The two officers who arrested me were in the front. Dawn was just starting to roll away the stone from the front of the cave. We were passing through a neighborhood I didn't know. No matter how many times I asked them, they wouldn't tell me where they were taking me. I was so frightened, my hands behind me like that. All the things I took for granted every day were gone. My control over my life was utterly gone, I couldn't even scratch my nose if it itched. I was being taken by strangers to an unknown location. They were real policemen, I knew that now. I couldn't believe they were going to kill me. I watched the view through the windshield like I was watching a movie through a chain link fence. Who knows how it will turn out? The only thing to do is watch, there's no alternative. The police car turned up a long driveway, weaving through a maze of sand colored, dreary block buildings. Wherever these bastards were taking me, it couldn't be worse than what I'd just been through.

Chapter 36

The ABCs Of Mule Training

Despite the common opinion, mules are easy to train. They have a reputation for being hard because they're stubborn, ornery, and willful. They're also breathtakingly stupid. But the secret to training them is simple. First you've got to get their attention. Once you do that, the rest flows naturally. And doing that is simpler than most people think.

First you find a nice, solid, two by four, a little bit longer than a baseball bat. Grip it firmly at one end and plant your feet. Swing it with all your might, crushing the business end between the mule's eyes. You now have its attention. Now the education can begin.

It's not a very flattering comparison, but I'm afraid it's accurate. That's what it took to wake me up. That's what it took to initiate the training process. And like a mule, I didn't learn fast, but I learned real good.

My moments spent in the back seat of a police car are over, if I have anything to say about it at all.

My days inside the locked wards of a mental hospital are over, unless I decide to admit myself.

I'm not letting this illness get away from me again, even if I have to seal myself in a timed bank vault to let an episode blow over.

The night I spent with those cops was just too much humiliation to ever relive. I turned myself over to them, I gave them Carte Blanche to mess me up and have fun with me as much as they wanted. They were mean enough, cheap enough, and scared enough, (the way all people are scared of crazy folk), to exploit it to the max. That's on me. I served myself up on a platter and they kicked me around like a soccer ball just because they were having a slow night. That's on me. I made myself a victim, I turned the power over to somebody else. In this case, a real cruel ramajama. That's on me. That's my mistake. But it's yesterday's papers I guarantee.

Anybody who wants to have power over me now is going to have to slap it out of my hands. I know it happens every day, but that doesn't mean I'm going to help. I've got a little fight in me after all, why should I make it easy for the bastards of the world? I didn't just help those cops, I practically told them to do it.

But of all of the humiliation of that night, this is the worst. Worse than being cuffed, kicked, and beaten by two professional bullies. Worse than standing in an interrogation room in nothing but my drawers while I was grilled, ridiculed, and scared to tears. Worse than having my person violated in ways I had never even imagined. Far worse.

The worst thing is, I owe them a debt of thanks. I know that they were sent by society to protect itself from me. The menace. But in doing that, they began the process of protecting me from me. They did it in a cruel way. They did it in an uneducated way. But they did it. Police after all, are the ones in the trenches. They're the ones on the front lines. Manic people are scary, and police are trained to expect the worst and deal with the worst. They didn't see a guy who would soon be having lunch at the White House with President Bush and B.B. King. And the Attorney General for that matter, although I didn't have a chance to chat with him. They saw a big guy with a car full of crap who looked psycho and talked hostile. They freaked. They panicked. They picked up the metaphorical two by four and whacked me right between the eyes. The high had hit its apex. The descent began. The descent which ultimately ended in safety and a second chance. I don't like to admit it but those bastards may have saved my life.

I've gotten a lot of training in the months and years that followed that awful night, and I've learned my lesson. Mental illness is a loaded gun, and it's not smart to court disaster. Life is dangerous enough as it is. I'm too old to be doing a bad Jean Paul Sartre impression. I've no plans to play Russian roulette with my future again. Self-destruction and suicide are the oldest, and saddest, stories in the Manic Depressive handbook. That's one cliché I'm hell-bent to avoid. I learned slow but I learned real good. No games no more.

My Afghani adventure might have been enough. It was a highly informative travelogue. My post-divorce descent into Hades was riveting, and the rivets were driven right into my stomach. Neither one got through. But Invisible Driving, complete with the trimmings, gave me all the schooling I needed.

The second step in my education was worse than the cops. The island of forgotten souls. Being locked down, locked up, struck down, doped up, put down, cooped up with the cracked, half-cracked, homeless, demented, most broken, saddest citizens I've ever laid eyes on was more than I could bear. I knew I didn't belong there. But I *was* there. So in at least one sense, I *did* belong there.

I felt the full weight of that wood again, right between my eyes.

Chapter 37

Caged Cat

The cops dropped me off at the zoo. The nuthouse. The loony bin. The laughing academy. The cracker factory. The funny farm. Apparently I was a few bricks shy of a load. The porch light was on but nobody was home. I had a cracked block. I wasn't playing with a full deck. I had bats in the belfry. I was riding on bald tires. One minute I was a free man, the next I was locked inside an insane asylum. I discovered myself undergoing intake procedures in a place called Pennsylvania Emergency Psychiatric Services, PEPS. I was vastly relieved to be out of handcuffs and no longer in the presence of the police. My mood turned quickly from terror to righteous indignation. As the pleasant, soft-spoken male counselor took down the needed information I raved on about how I was going to destroy the police who had put me here. I was going to get them thrown off the force. I was going to sue them. The grand, larger than life feeling of power was returning, I felt as though I was now talking to a reasonable person who would side with me.

When he was satisfied that he had all the information he needed he asked if I wanted him to call anybody for me. I thought for a second and then gave him Sarah's number. She would know to call my father and brother, she had their numbers, and she needed to know what was happening because Paula needed to know where I was. It was horrible, embarrassing and horrible, but I needed to mobilize every resource I had to get out as quickly as possible. The idea of being confined was anathema. I was the guy who never stopped walking, never stopped moving, all of the Dakotas were not big enough to contain my energy.

In one sense, all my problems had disappeared in an instant. I no longer had to worry about which to become a success at first, performance artist, blues singer, lounge lizard, etc. There certainly wasn't much I could do to free James Brown from the inside of PEPS. I was suddenly free of all difficult choices, decisions. Now I had only one focus, get out of this madhouse as soon as possible. And within that focus there was only one subset, make my time here tolerable. I knew that being cooped up would make me nazzbat unless I labored to make it somehow bearable, even pleasant. So, the one-man variety show was back in business, working the hardest room of his career. But at least there was one good thing about it, I definitely had a captive audience.

I was led into an examination room. Under constant supervision I was told to take a shower and change into green hospital togs, those shapeless one size fits all garments with no buttons, zippers or buckles, just cords to be tied in bows. For the first time in months I had no pockets to stuff. No paraphernalia to play with. No idiosyncratic oddities to instantly demonstrate to anyone who should care to notice that I was different, creative, special. Man qua man. No accessories to telegraph social position. With the exception of some drab green fabric hanging limply and shapelessly around me I was as unencumbered as the day I was jettisoned, twitching and screaming, into this world, if considerably larger. In some respects it was quite liberating. Zero. Nothing to fidget with. Nothing to lock. Nothing to pick up or straighten. Each person I encountered I interviewed as much as they interviewed me. I was going to become the most popular patient in the ward. I remembered everybody's name. One of the attendants was Israeli, I trotted out my favorite Yiddish words for him. I was determined to manifest hyper-competence so these people would quickly realize the mistake that had taken place and release me.

I was given a handful of pills and some orange juice to wash them down. Two very large attendants escorted me down a long hallway, a long hallway which looked exactly like a prison hallway all protestations notwithstanding, and locked me in a small room. "So no one else will bother you," one of them said. Relentlessly resourceful, McHarg has found himself a new home without even trying. Warm, safe from the elements, waited on hand and foot. Whatever they'd given me began to tug on me like an anchor. My jitteriness slacked off, I was floating, falling, dropping in slow motion like a pilot without a parachute who's leapt from an injured aircraft. All my weariness began to accumulate, gathering force, pulling at me with its own, strange gravity. How good it feels to let go. Eyes closed, I could see earth way down below me, an oddly colorful marble rolling across a black stone floor. That was once my home. The earth grew larger. Mercifully I was dead asleep before the moment of impact.

I woke up when one of the attendants opened my door and said, "Dinnertime." Groggy and dazed I followed him down the hall and around the corner. He left me at the end of a line of people waiting to enter a door and thus I was introduced to my fellow bedlamites. There was a complete cross-sampling. Mostly white, some black. Mostly young, some middle-aged, some old. Some seemed normal, others were obviously fucked up. One bear of a man complete with great, bushy beard stood in the back of the dining room and rocked, his feet planted firmly in one place. He was holding the receiver of a pay phone to his ear, not saying a word into it. He stared blankly ahead. I watched him.

A wiry young man standing next to me in line, waiting for his food, turned to me and said, "See that? He's not talking to anybody. That phone doesn't work." Right away I liked this young man. We introduced ourselves. His name was Mike. I felt better already. We sat together at the table. I was glad that I didn't have to endure my first meal alone. I ate the food. It was horrible, but well balanced. I realized that it had been ages since I'd sat down to a complete meal like this, with all the food groups dutifully represented. Claire never cooked and I'd stopped eating at restaurants when my money had given out. Every once in while I'd stop into a convenience store and get some milk and orange juice. I'd been subsisting like that for a long time. I was being roped back into the mainstream. Regular meals were part of the process.

After dinner I was introduced to the smoking ritual. There was a common room at the other end of the hall. It had a pool table, a ping pong table, a few tables and chairs, a radio, and some stand-up ashtrays. There were windows made of glass blocks, impossible to break. Looking through these blocks gave the world outside a wobbly, blurred, distorted face. One got the impression of trees and clouds without actually being able to see them. Smoking was permitted only during the last fifteen minutes of every hour so at quarter 'til whatever there was a stampede to this room and those who had cigarettes readied them and those who didn't begged them or pulled butts out of the ashtrays. Then an attendant would appear at the doorway and light one of the cigarettes. We were not allowed to have matches. Once that first cigarette was lit, fire passed through the room like a rumor in a financially unstable company. The person with a lit cigarette would use his cigarette to give a light to a couple of people, they would do likewise, until in scant moments the entire room was engulfed in smoke like some sort of fathers' waiting area in the maternity ward of a hospital from yesteryear. Everybody smoked.

I was sitting next to Mike, taking all this in. I asked the obvious question. "So, why are you in here?"

Pulling deeply on his cigarette he said in a soft voice, "I tried to kill myself." I was shocked, he seemed like such a likeable guy.

Without thinking that it was a rude question I asked, "How?"

Not even pausing he replied, "I ran in front of a car, it was a Bronco." I was really set back. I've been low in my day, but I've never attempted suicide. Already I cared about this man's pain, it didn't seem right.

Considerations of tact far behind, I just asked, "Why?"

"You know," he said, "so many people have asked me that, I wrote a list of reasons." With jerky, nervous movements he removed a crumpled piece of paper from his jeans, brushed it smooth, and handed it to me. I read this resumé from hell in utter horror. Abandoned by his parents. A string of foster homes. Abuse, including sexual abuse, before the age of ten. Male prostitution before age fourteen. Alcoholism and heroin addiction before sixteen. Years as a petty thief resulting in many stints in juvenile homes and finally a two year stretch in prison. A busted marriage with a wife who'd left him and taken his young son, disappearing completely. When I was done reading I returned the document to him, humbled by the agony he'd endured, humbled by my relative good fortune.

He smiled a thin, wistful smile. "So now when people ask me why I'm unhappy, I just say, that's why." In some strange way I felt honored that he'd shared this information with me. One of the attendants came over and informed me that I had a phone call. I walked down the hall to where the payphones were.

It was my ex-wife Sarah. She told me that she'd called Claire, my dad, and my brother and explained the situation. Perhaps I did something good in a past life, I thought, or I've something good yet to do in this one, because as ex-wives go, Sarah can certainly be an ace when she wants to be. She told me that she'd explained to Paula that I was in the hospital, did I want to speak to her? Of course I said that I did.

I heard that thin, high-pitched, seven-year-old girl voice. It was quivering. "Hi daddy."

Just the lilt was such music, it lifted my soul up off the floor. "Hi sweetheart," I began to bubble. "Gosh, I miss you so much, I love you." It was going to be all right.

"I love you, daddy," the voice was really quivering now, and then her composure gave out. She began sniffling and crying. I didn't know what to say. I had screwed up so badly, there was no point in trying to con my daughter into believing that everything was fine. Everything wasn't fine.

"I'm sorry, daddy," she said in between sobs. "I really want to talk to you, but I can't right now, I'm too upset." She sobbed.

"That's all right, that's all right," I hastened to assure her. Sarah came back on the line, said a quick goodbye, and the line was dead.

Very gingerly, carefully, gently, I rested the receiver back in its chrome cradle. I was completely overwhelmed by Paula. What an astounding degree of sophistication from a seven-year-old girl. She loved me, she missed me, she wanted to tell me about it, but she was too upset to get the words out. But in the midst of all that hurt, that fear, she still found the resolve to apologize to me. Because she knew I needed to hear from her and she didn't want to let me down. So she apologized for her inability to hold up her end of the conversation. Me, the guy who had let her down in so many ways, who instead of reading her a bedtime story was wasting his time in a bughouse, she was apologizing to me. What had I done to deserve such an amazing daughter? I felt blessed. If I had any doubt about my desire to cope for my own sake, I had no doubt about my desire to do it for her. I was connected to the rest of the world after all. I wasn't merely watching a movie. I wasn't floating freely in space. My actions, my very state of being itself, had an effect on other people.

Obviously something was wrong or I wouldn't be in this nightmare. And just as obviously I was going to shovel as much coal as I had to, to fix whatever it was that was wrong. That fragile, tiny voice was a siren song I couldn't resist. From the look of it, the facts weren't very pretty. But, as Sarah used to say, where there's a will there's relatives. Paula, that pint-sized jumble of unguarded emotions, needed me to do the right thing. Embarrassed, ashamed of myself, feeling deficient in every way imaginable, I squeezed back the tears that wanted to wash down my face.

Chapter 38

Light And Fog

The cops had done a job, they'd done a job on my head. They'd literally knocked some sense into me. The fantasies of Mania were starting to dissolve, transforming into ether, wafting away in the breeze. I began to see my life with a clear, scientific eye.

Talking to my daughter on the phone did a job too. It did a job on my heart. I was moved by real feelings again, not the preposterous false feelings of Mania.

The illness had crowded out mental and emotional truth. As they ebbed back in, I could see the work I needed to do. The very thought of it made me feel weary and unequipped.

I was especially weak in the heart department. When it came to knowing and telling my feelings, I was barely out of diapers. Being a father *had* helped me a lot, I'd been making a good bit of headway. My little girl wore her heart on her sleeve, that forced me to face it. In the course of raising her, loving her, caring for her, I'd learned that handling emotions is not like handling snakes. Emotions are more likely to kill you if you *don't* touch them than if you do.

But getting down in the kitchen where the action is wasn't yet one of my showcase attributes. I still had some pretty gritty emotional housecleaning yet to do.

In that desolate building, my heart's feelings materialized like dream characters, appearing gradually, emerging through the chill of a thick, ghostly fog. Like phantoms melting through a curtain of gauze.

Specters. Huge, undeniable. Striding slowly in snow falling as gently as angel tears, their black, ragged cloaks growing white and wet. Absolute stillness surrounding them, the hush of reverie. Mouths blowing plumes of steam into the air, the breath of soundless words. Dignified, enduring, patient. Doleful, ghastly, magnificent. Phantasms of such force, such force and solemnity.

Terror. Loneliness. Shame.

Anguish. Sadness. Guilt.

Emptiness.

I saw all this through the fog, in the sunken eye sockets of the specters. I saw all this in myself, I couldn't lie anymore. Those were moments of crippling sorrow. Moments of epiphany.

I was one of them. I was one of them too. Walking in the silence. Wearing a coat of snow. At last listening. At last dumb. At last still.

We were all ghosts in that place of suffering, walking dead, each one of us wearing his pain like a garment, a white jacket, a straight jacket.

I've lived with the saddest people in the world, aristocrats of the soul. I've lived with them, and I've been one of them. It gave me common wisdom. It taught me that we're all in this together. We're all equal. If we don't love one another and help one another then we're no better than the worms who will ultimately be having the last laugh on us anyway.

But even though I knew and understood, I wasn't yet ready to confess that I was just another specter. The trip down from a Manic high is not an express elevator ride from the delights of the penthouse to the facts and fighting of the ground floor. It's also not a smooth, downwardly tilting line, it doesn't look like a corporate sales chart for a bad quarter. It's full of smaller and smaller peaks and valleys, like a mountain range gradually slumping, sloping at last to the level of the sea.

My Manic way of denying that I belonged in the nuthouse was by being super sane, super competent, super cooperative. One attendant later said, "Alistair put on quite a show." And put on a show I did. The Catskill comic in a loony bin. But the staff was too smart, they'd seen Manics in action before. They knew I was trying to fool them, and myself, with the "model patient" routine. They weren't buying it. It was just another variation of the old Manic, "I'm fine everything's fine and I'm gonna prove it. Well yes I'm in a loony bin but that's just for the moment and actually I'm fine everything's fine and I'm gonna prove it."

Only time, that wounder of all heels, time and Lithium, with a couple of hits of Thorazine mixed in, would do it.

The cops were the front line. These guys were the second line. It was a humiliating and frightening place to be, I was captive and claustrophobic as hell, but it worked. They did their best to bring me in for a smooth landing, like air traffic controllers talking down an F-14 piloted by a Tasmanian devil.

Chapter 39

Lifestyles Of The Poor And Psychotic

Getting a laugh out of a homeless person is difficult, but breaking up a roomful of suicidal welfare cases challenged my abilities to the limit. I managed with an act I called, "Lifestyles Of The Poor And Psychotic." There's a television program which showcases the excesses of rich people. It's hosted by an obnoxious man named Robin Leach, what a wonderfully appropriate name for him, who yells in his high pitched Cockney accent as he fawns over yachts, estates, luxury automobiles et al, as though the ability to waste money ostentatiously in an orgy of hedonistic self-gratification was somehow interesting and clever in itself. The name of the show is Lifestyles Of The Rich And Famous. So, with Mike as my primary audience, I created, Lifestyles Of The Poor And Psychotic. In rapid-fire Robin Leach delivery I described our life at PEPS as Robin Leach might.

"Here they are in their fabulous game room, lavishly appointed with pool and ping-pong tables, doing the Thorazine shuffle. Notice how their feet never leave the floor." They had put me on Lithium, the magic potion which they give to Manic Depressives, so I was gradually becoming less hyper, and even though I was on Thorazine too I still had a considerable amount of energy. "A lovely walk in the woods provides a pleasing interlude for these pioneers of psychiatric frontiers." There was indeed a nature trail and if you were well behaved you got to go on closely supervised group walks. I quickly dubbed it the

Psycho Path. "Food, food, and more food is what you'll find in this gourmet cafeteria. Convenience is the watchword here. Only the finest plastic utensils are used to avoid any accidental disembowelings. Sturdy metal trays keep the elements of the meals neatly divided into precise nutritional groupings." The food was awful but there was plenty of it, my appetite started to return.

"In the outside world when you invite a group of friends over for a session of lying, denying, bombastic bragging, and neurotic whining, it's called a cocktail party. But here, it's called group therapy. And to make sure everyone gets a turn, there's even a group leader who laps up these sordid sagas like caviar." Actually I liked group. I'd never done group therapy before and it was in group that I said for the first time, I'm Manic Depressive. It felt good to confess, to give the illness a name. I admitted a flaw and amazingly, the world did not come to an end. "Whether your pleasure is drifting up, up, and away in a beautiful balloon or what you fancy is a few steps down, down, down the dark ladder, it all happens twice a day at Med Time. See them line up for pill popping action that spells mood satisfaction time and time again." There are many ways to take drugs in this society and some of them are legal. Happily, Lithium is not a pharmaceutical as such but a naturally occurring salt.

"And how do these aristocrats of oddness settle down after a busy day of counting their fingers and slashing their wrists with plastic forks? It might be in the security of a supervised single cell like this, or more likely, in the warm, dorm-like atmosphere of a six-person suite where a symphony of snoring provides a soothing backdrop. Can't sleep? No bother. Here at PEPS attendants are in the halls twenty-four hours a day, always eager to discuss pressing issues like, are there or are there not flying dogs in the building eating brain tissue?" Reality, what a concept.

One young man tried to slash his wrists with a plastic fork. A doomed, pseudo biker who was heavily sedated and rambled on and on about Metallica, his favorite heavy metal rock group.

I felt badly for him for being so desperate but I felt even worse for him for being such an idiot. The more it hurts, the funnier it gets.

My caseworker explained the deal to me. He was an extremely agreeable, if overworked, young guy. The police had initiated an involuntary commitment. That lasted for three days. I was stunned by their right to control my fate. Then there was a review, done by the physician at PEPS. If he thought I was all right, I would be released. If not, they could keep me longer. I had no power over the situation at all. To make things worse, like they needed to get worse, the cops had filed charges against me which would be waiting when I finally did get out. Sometimes, he said, when there was a diagnosis of mental illness, the cops would drop the charges. In fact, in a case like this, that's what usually happened. But not here.

"You must have really pissed them off," the caseworker said. It was hard to stay optimistic. I was captive in an insane asylum and facing criminal charges when I finally got out.

Getting visitors, having people on the outside rooting for me, helped a lot. I soon realized that many of the people in with me had nobody on the outside who had the desire or the ability to help. Claire was the first. God I was glad to see her. I apologized profusely for my behavior. We talked about my illness. I was on my medication now, I was getting better. I told her about the cops. Claire, as anti-establishment as they come, was sympathetic. She acknowledged that, perhaps, if I promised to stay on the medication, it would be all right for me to move back in. She felt partially responsible in that she had thrown me out but she said she was afraid, she didn't know what else to do. I was quick to forgive her of course. I was nuts, plain and simple. I'd lost it, the pressure had gotten to me. All I wanted was my freedom back. I didn't want to be cooped up with people who asked me questions like, "Are you the King Lobster?" and, "Did Satan call for me while I was in the bathroom?" I could try to make it fun by charming the nurses and the pretty, young assistants who led aerobics classes and took us on walks, but the cold fact of it was I was going barzonic being locked up. And now that the Lithium level was starting to rise in my blood and I was becoming less hyper, I was able to see reality again. I really was in a mental institution, this was no movie, no joke. I really wasn't seeing my daughter, my blood. I really was facing criminal charges. The more I began to see my real situation, the more desperate I was to do something about it.

The next visitor was my brother Malcolm. I told him about my place. He said that he would call the landlord to let him in and get a friend to help him move the remaining stuff out. He'd store it at my father's. There was room in the barn. He'd take care of getting my car back from the police. Malcolm the doctor knows all about illnesses and about developing strategies to cure them. He's much younger than me but now he was the adult, I was the mixed-up kid. He's married, stable, responsible, people trust him with their lives for Chrissake. I was incapable of performing the simple feat of staying out of trouble with the authorities. We're close, and he had some awareness of my first episode, so I didn't feel that horrible facing him in my reduced circumstances. And I was immensely grateful for his support, his presence. I was becoming reconnected to the world of other people. It hurt but it felt good at the same time.

The tough one was my father. He looked ludicrously out of place in the recreation room. The very picture of a visiting Oxford Don clad in well-tailored tweed, surrounded by people who through no fault of their own were poor, bent, insane, and degraded. They eyed him curiously.

I was told later, "Your dad is quite a classy guy."

One young man said bitterly to me after seeing my father, "This is just an excursion for you. For me, it's a life."

I had to give him credit for rising to the occasion. He'd talked to the police to try to get them to drop the charges. He said he would pay for me to see a psychiatrist until I was back on my feet again and could support myself. It was difficult for him. He hurt for me but it was hard for him to understand what had happened. It's one thing to lose a job, quite another to come apart. But he gave me the supreme kindness of not being accusatory. He wanted to know if I was all right, if I was being treated well, and what he could do. He didn't have a lot of money to make the problem vanish. There was no talk of a high priced lawyer to make everything go away. Besides, the law was on the side of the keepers. I would have to convince them I was not a threat to myself or to society before they released me. They had the power to hold me. But the main thing was, he was there. My mother, if she were still alive, would have been happy to know that when the dikes broke and the dark sea raged across my landscape, my father and brother were there with sandbags.

I was in PEPS for ten days, the longest ten days of my life. I bounced off the walls like the silver ball in an old fashioned pinball machine. I hustled, I charmed, I knew absolutely everybody there by name. I became the house mascot. Singing, telling jokes, obeying every rule, sympathetically listening to the woes of the other patients. After a while I felt like I was running the group therapy sessions. At last the head head doctor decided that my Lithium level was high enough. I was sleeping through the night, something that hadn't happened in months. I had a place to go, Claire was going to give me another chance. I had a psychiatrist I was going to see when I got out who would continue my treatment. In sum, I had a plan.

Claire picked me up on the morning of the tenth day. It was a wild, March day, the clouds swirled in a maze of dark grays, brilliant white, and foreboding black. I was euphoric, thrilled to be alive, thrilled to be free again, thrilled to hold and kiss Claire again. I wanted to do everything twice in ten minutes. Life was glorious, wonderful. We drove quickly home and made love with a greedy hunger and delight that can only come from deprivation.

Chapter 40

The Long Walk Home

Years ago. Teheran. Ate opium. Spent whole day hotel room. Didn't move. Didn't even smoke cigarettes. Stared out window. Listened to guts of ceiling fan bang against case. Bangs, whirs, clanks, silent bits. Fascinating. Dreadful. Boring. Time stopped. Release. Nothing. Sweet, sexy, allure of death. Huge void cut me off from all that wasn't me. Aloof. Removed. World of objects, tasks, not my world. Like that now.

Hell with extra cheese. Shrink loaded me up with Thorazine, Lithium. Feel like five fat people sitting on me. Eyelids heavy as fire curtains. In Claire's back room, my room, I'm great lump. So swacked, barely stay awake. Days on floor. Covered with my junk. Papers, photos, room looks like hamster cage. Move by sliding on butt, push path through mess. Don't want to talk to nobody. A few calls, Sarah, Malcolm, dad. Otherwise, only talk to Claire. Can't be strong anymore, sad, blue, sorry to be me. Can't see Paula, they say I'd scare her. Gloom, guilt. Left a trail of trash behind. Can't see Zelda, Hilary again. Hate me. Lost my place. Owe landlord a zillion dollars. Up on charges. Could go to jail. Need lawyer. No job, no money, owe everybody. Electric bills, phone bills, credit card bills. Credit rating trashed. Need Claire for roof over head. House, Claire, look different now. No castle, dump. Worst part, lucky to have it. Claire. Still like her art, rest so pitiful. Her stupid philosophy. Ashamed of being female. Loves to live in shit, chaos, trash. Like her, but no.

Tear away stupid vanities, dead skin. Not keeper of kittens. Brute. Woman user. Not performance artist. Out of control Manic, thinks he's funny. James Brown still in jail. Not soul singer, street singer. Not King Lounge Lizard. Lonely man, waste time, money in bars. No reptile, human being. Lousy father. Cripple. Can't take care of self. Fool. Dilettante. No-talent chickenshit. Looneybird. Gonna be crazy forever. Too much weight. Can't get up. Want to give up. Want to give up. Fuck it.

Push up off of floor. I weigh a thousand pounds. I'm dizzy goddamnit. Push legs, stand. I'm ten feet tall. Whoaa, sit in chair. Elbows on desk, hands hold chin. Spread feet, won't fall over. Need paper, need pencil. What am I doing? Oh yeah, that's right. Make list, things must do. New job. Beat charges. Pay bills. Paula back. Get own place. See friends. Goddamnit, can't even write this shit, how will I ever do it? Don't feel well enough to shave, how can I look for new job? Goddamnit, fuck. Got to start. Call old friend in biz. Get leads. Open address book. Find first number. Pick up receiver. Hmmmmmmmmmmmmmmm. Numbers on phone swimming around, stop it! You can you dizzy motherfucker, you can beat it. You can, you can. Think it enough, make it true. Push the button. Push. Push the button. Push. Push. Push. Push.

Chapter 41

The Nicer The Nice, The Higher The Price

In Claire's house, I found my absolute zero, my personal skid row. The crash was complete. I was face down on the floor. My head was stuffed with cotton wool, I didn't know what day of the week it was. I struggled to hang on to consciousness like a mountain climber scratching an escarpment with ragged fingernails in a desperate attempt to escape falling, falling to a certain death. The Thorazine had knocked me out like a heavyweight champion. I had nothing, nothing but shame. Regaining control of my life looked impossible.

Deciding to get up off that floor required every scrap of resolve in my entire being. It was nothing less than a decision to live. Had I not had my daughter to live for, I'm not certain I could have managed. I chose to live, knowing full well that the weeks and months ahead of me would hold nothing but painful reminders and ugly struggle. I chose to live, surrounded by evidence that I didn't have the wherewithal to manage. I chose to live, even though my faith in myself was completely shattered. As I pushed my body onto the chair, like a man pushing a piece of Jello across a plate with a feather, I pulled myself out of the grave. Somewhere inside there was still a microscopic beacon of hope, I don't know why. There was a little grit, too, thank goodness. Even though my soul ached to surrender, to give up, I found ten cc of courage. Not much, but enough to get me started.

Making a phone call is such a trivial, pedestrian activity. But for me, at that moment, it was heavy with significance. I was reaching out to the real world for the first time in many months, reestablishing contact. I was taking that first step, the hardest one. The first step on a journey of a thousand miles.

Hitting absolute zero is an experience I wouldn't wish on anyone. And yet, for me, it was unavoidable. My response to it changed me profoundly. Changed me in ways that transformed my life. The battle gave me my character, my strength. I had grown up with a lot of arrogance, learned from a real master, my father. Battling this illness forced me to shed my arrogance and assume a healthy measure of humility. After all, I had found a beast in the jungle too big for me to kill alone. I had to study Manic Depression, I had to learn how to defeat it. I was forced to admit that I needed help.

Getting used to the idea of asking for help came slowly. Both my parents were rugged individualists, very self-sufficient. I imagined that I was too, although I never had their competence. But Manic Depression introduced me to the idea of a support network, a network that was there to save my life. A psychologist, for the emotional stuff. A psychiatrist, for the medication. Getting beyond the shame and admitting my illness to friends and family so that they became part of the solution. Understanding employers. On and on.

Me, the solitary poet, brooding in a tower, forced, absolutely forced into the arms of other people just to survive. Irony of ironies. Ultimately, gift of gifts. Because now I see what I was missing, what I was too afraid to touch. The love of others, the caring and concern. Feeling connected to it, and so grateful for it, makes me want to give back in return. When I do, I discover just how much I have to give.

Something had to break the cycle of selfishness and insecurity. The illness did. That was a blessing.

I'd spent years after my divorce struggling to achieve independence. I equated it with manhood. I was proud that I'd managed, I felt like I didn't need anyone. Because I'd been such a pampered pooch coming up, learning this lesson was hugely important for me. The Mania that followed my divorce had driven me to a shrink. He kept me on Lithium for a couple of years. But I got tired of him, he was a lousy shrink and he was costing me a fortune. I went off Lithium. I drifted in and out of hypomanic episodes, but there was never anything serious enough to make me get help. My cocky attitude returned. I had it together. I stood on my own. I reasoned that the shrink and the medicine had just been a way to get me through a bad patch. I was again, Sir Alistair the Solitary.

That was a mistake, which I will never make again.

Unlearning my devotion to self-sufficiency was tough, but there wasn't an alternative. For me, the best independence is knowing where and when to go for help. Nobody can do everything alone. We all rely on others for something. I rely on others for my sanity.

Fear of failing, fear of dreaming, fear of living, these fears have been burned out of me. I've been purified by fire. From too high to too low and back again, again and again, now I spend my time solidly in the middle. As aware of my strengths as I am of my weaknesses. Focused on what's real. Surrounding myself with people I love, and people who love me. Putting myself in situations that are nourishing, healing, and challenging. I've spent so much of my life lying in the shadows. First, the shadow of my larger-than-life father. Next, the shadow of death, my mother's death, which hung like a pall, silencing the music in my heart. Then, the shadow of a mysterious mental illness, a frightening, bizarre disability.

Well, that's it for the shadows. I refuse to be defined by my illness just as I refuse to be defined by my father's reputation. Today I walk like a man, as good as any other man. I have as much right to be proud of myself as anyone else. I keep my back straight and I hold my head high. I smile at the sky. At last, at last I'm smiling. I'm stronger and gentler than ever before. More confident. Humbler. More ambitious. And completely without shame.

Doing an excellent job of just being myself looks like more than enough to keep me happily occupied for the rest of my life.

I'm out of the underworld, out of the shadows. Now I cast a shadow of my own.

Made in the USA